FOOD
FOR TOMORROW?

FOOD
FOR TOMORROW?

C. Dean Freudenberger

AUGSBURG Publishing House • Minneapolis

FOOD FOR TOMORROW?

Copyright © 1984 Augsburg Publishing House

All rights reserved. Except for brief quotations in critical articles or reviews, no part of this book may be reproduced in any manner without prior written permission from the publisher. Write to: Permissions, Augsburg Publishing House, 426 S. Fifth St., Box 1209, Minneapolis MN 55440.

Scripture quotations unless otherwise noted are from the Revised Standard Version of the Bible, copyright 1946, 1952, and 1971 by the Division of Christian Education of the National Council of Churches.

Library of Congress Cataloging in Publication Data

Freudenberger, C. Dean, 1930-
  FOOD FOR TOMORROW?

  Bibliography: p. 167
  1. Agriculture — Planning. 2. Land use, Rural — Planning. 3. Soil conservation—Planning. 4. Agriculture—Environmental aspects—Planning. 5. Food supply—Planning. I. Title.
HD1415.F69 1984   338.1'9   83-72119
ISBN 0-8066-2063-3 (pbk.)

Manufactured in the U.S.A.   APH 10-2333

1 2 3 4 5 6 7 8 9 0 1 2 3 4 5 6 7 8 9

Contents

Preface

Will there be food tomorrow? How can we best care for the land which serves as the base for all of life? These questions have captured my imagination and energies for more than 35 years.

As a boy of 14 I helped my father and uncle do fertilizer trials in the Imperial, Coachella, and San Joaquin Valleys of California. I became involved in American agriculture during the advent of agricultural chemicals, long before the idea had been generally accepted.

In 1950, during the third year of my college training in agriculture at the California State Polytechnic University at San Luis Obispo, I was first confronted with the growing worldwide need for more food. I was invited to serve as an agricultural missionary in Africa to help introduce beef cattle in the Katanga province of what was then the Belgian Congo and to work for the expansion of indigenous vegetable and tree production.

Before jumping into this work, I undertook four years of additional study in philosophy, theology, and ethics, including a year of study in Brussels in language, cultural anthropology, and colonial law. Here we discussed global food shortages, the environmental impact of temperate-zone agricultural technologies in the tropical world, fossil fuel shortages — topics never touched on in American agricultural colleges at that time.

During the next 17 years, from 1956 to 1973, I served as an agriculturalist in the Belgian Congo (now Zaire) and then as the agricultural program officer for the World Division of the General Board of Global Ministries of the United Methodist Church.

In 1969 I completed doctoral studies in social ethics, political philosophy, the economics of agricultural development, and environmental issues. I also served as a rural community and agricultural development trainer for 13 French-speaking West African Peace Corps training programs. My work took me to more than 60 food-deficit nations of Africa, Asia, Latin America, and the Pacific islands. I attended the United Nations World Food Conference in Rome in 1973 and the UN World Conference on Desertification in Nairobi in 1976. During these years I gained a global perspective on the entire spectrum of ecojustice issues, particularly regarding food and agriculture.

Since 1973 I have been professor of international development studies and the world mission of the church at the School of Theology in Claremont, California. I work with graduate students from all over the globe and colleagues in all theological disciplines. We struggle with the question about food for tomorrow, and we search the biblical wisdom for a new perspective on the land, and on agriculture, and on the relationship of humanity to all of life.

In my life and thought, biblical wisdom, theology, and ethics are integrated with firsthand experience in agriculture on the global scale. From this perspective I have written books and journal articles on the problems of agriculture and ecology. These include *Christian Responsibility in a Hungry World*, coauthored with Paul Minus (Abingdon, 1975) and the filmstrip series *A World Hungry, The Churches in Rural Development* and *The Gift of Land: Biblical Perspectives on a Threatened World*. I have contributed chapters to *Beyond Survival*, edited by Dieter Hessel (Friendship Press, 1977), *Farming the Lord's Land*, edited by Charles Lutz (Augsburg, 1980), and *The Causes of Hunger*, edited by William Bryon (Orbis, 1982).

This present book, *Food for Tomorrow?*, was written while I was on a sabbatical research leave in Cambridge, England, including travel in Scandinavia, Sicily, Kenya, and Upper

Volta. In it I again draw on my practical experience in world agriculture and my study of theology to seek new perspectives on the problems of world hunger, land use, and ecological issues.

In Part 1, "The World Food Crisis," we will look at the "normative design" of the fragile ecosystem and the magnitude of the stress now being placed on it. This includes issues of land use, soil loss, water and air pollution, and political and economic realities.

Part 2, "The Needed Ethic for a New Agriculture," looks to the biblical wisdom of the Old and New Testaments as a source for a new agricultural ethic based on the guidelines of justice, participation, and sustainability.

Part 3, "Toward Solution," outlines some of the solutions to the problem of agriculture now being attempted in various parts of the world. It suggests needed reforms and identifies areas for further research. The final chapter suggests some ways that Christian churches can contribute to the solution of the problem of agriculture.

Acknowledgments

This book was written at the invitation extended to me from Augsburg Publishing House. I am grateful for this challenge because it encouraged me to do some serious reflection on the future of American agriculture and the world food crisis.

I wish to express appreciation to the administration, faculty, and trustees of the School of Theology at Claremont, its library staff, and to the Greenville Foundation, who made my research leave possible so that this book could be developed. A special word of thanks is extended to our faculty secretary, Sharlene Jensen, for the countless hours spent at the typewriter during the preparation of this manuscript for the publisher. I am grateful to my family for their ceaseless encouragements and particularly to my wife, who gave so much of her time and skill to bibliographical research and development. We hope that this book will be useful for all who struggle for food for today and for tomorrow.

PART 1

The World Food Crisis

There may be no more important social problem in this
century than the increasing imbalance between
human population and the resource base that sustains
it. The problem is creeping, diffuse, and undramatic
compared with others that command attention: nuclear
proliferation, international monetary disturbances,
or the politics of the Mid-East.

DONNELLA MEADOWS

1 The World in Crisis

Since the dawn of civilization, one-half of the earth's food-producing soil has disappeared.

By the year 2000 one-third of the remaining soil will be lost.

Deserts will spread over every continent, including North America. Every year a land area the size of Luxembourg (200,000-300,000 hectares) is lost through desertification.

By the end of this century, less than five percent of the earth's surface will remain arable.

In the same period, by A.D. 2000, our global population will exceed six billion.

In the United States four million acres of arable land are being lost each year.

Each year in the United States we lose four billion tons of soil from wind and water erosion, a loss greater than that experienced during the tragic Dust Bowl disaster of the 1930s.

In the United States during the past 30 years, nearly four million farms and ranches have disappeared, and 30 million people have left the land. This is the greatest human migration in recorded history.

In the United States the increase in crop yield from chemical fertilizers peaked in 1975. Before the year 2050 our crop yields are expected to decline by 15-30%.

World forest resources are disappearing. Each year forests covering areas half the size of California are destroyed. By the year 2000, 40 percent of the remaining forest cover in the less-developed nations will be gone.

Former Secretary of Agriculture Bob Bergland declared, "We are on a collision course with disaster."

Facts like these reveal the magnitude and the urgency of the crisis in world agriculture, a crisis affecting all the people of the entire globe. This crisis is more radical and more serious than any other we face—except perhaps the possibility of nuclear annihilation.

Radical change in our relationship to the land, to the world ecosystem, is urgent. And change is possible.

In order to make this change a reality, we must first change our minds about the land and our relationship to it. We need to understand the fragile nature of our global system and the magnitude of the stress we have placed on it.

The normative design of the global system

Out of what we can call a primordial chaos an orderly world was created. Out of darkness came light. The sun is the source of all energy and the potential source of annihilation. Life on earth can survive the sun's heat only because of the delicate complex system of mechanisms which control the temperatures on earth. These systems have been developed over a period of more than 4.5 billion years. It is within this context of the delicate balances of creation that the magnitude of the global agricultural problem must be measured.

Earth is a relatively small planet. To us it seems large, yet the biosphere is so thin as to be virtually transparent. If we could reduce the earth to the size of a billiard ball, its mountainous surface would appear ivory smooth. We might be able to recognize the continents, but the oceans would be mere films of dampness, and we would not be able to detect any signs of life.[1]

One of our most precious resources is water. Of the earth's fresh water, more than 99% is retained in the ice caps and glaciers or is underground. Less than 1% is in lakes, rivers, and soil and therefore available for the support of human life and its technologies for producing food and fiber.

Within this thin biosphere, each living thing depends on a constant flow of energy from the sun. This energy must pass through three biological levels. One consists of the green plants which receive energy from the sun and fix it in the form of food for themselves and for all other living things. This level includes the aquatic phytoplankton. The second level consists of all animal life. No animals can fix solar energy. Animals must eat either plants or other animals that have themselves eaten plants. Thus, plants are producers of energy, and animals are consumers. The third level consists of organisms called "reducers," the microscopic life in the soil, such as the fungi and bacteria, that break down dead plants and animals and release their components to the cycles of the whole biosphere.[2]

This dependent and interdependent cycle of life has a history that stretches back to the moment of creation. All life in the biosphere—hummingbirds and dandelions, elephants and redwoods, people and squids—shares a common origin and a common destiny.

The magnitude of stress on the global system

In 1972 the United Nations Environmental Program (UNEP) was created by the General Assembly. The purpose of UNEP is to function as "the environmental conscience of the United Nations." Its task is to:

> Keep under review the world environmental situation in order to insure that emerging environmental problems of wide international significance receive appropriate and adequate consideration by governments.[3]

The UNEP *Annual Reviews* on "The State of the Environment" reveal the magnitude of stress on the earth's fragile ecosystem and show what is being done in response to this problem.

In 1976 the first *Annual Review* pointed out that humanity does not deliberately damage its own environment any more than a rational person would purposely destroy his or her own home. But when we act to satisfy our needs—when we grow food, raise cattle, build roads, or establish industries—our activities often produce side effects which are environmentally harmful. Sometimes these side effects make it difficult or even impossible to sustain the original activities.[4] The 1978 *Annual Review* adds:

> In the long evolution of the human race on this planet, a stage has been reached at which, through the rapid acceleration of science and technology, humanity has acquired the power to transform its environment in countless ways and on an unprecedented scale. The fact is that the human species has but this one planet on which to live, that the biosphere which surrounds it is fragile and easily damaged, and that humanity must work with its environment and not against it. Here begin new efforts to unite the nations of the world in a new and common purpose.[5]

UNEP suggests that environmental management is a twofold operation. First, the task is to identify where environmental degradation and resource depletion are making it difficult to meet basic human needs for food, shelter, health, clothing, education, and work. Second, the task is to modify human activities so as to eliminate undesirable side effects, while at the same time satisfying basic human needs on a sustainable basis.[6]

But the problem today is a confrontation between rising aspirations of a growing world population and the physical and ecological constraints of the biosphere. Consequently, this confrontation has brought humankind face to face with the outer limits of what the planet can provide.

The six UNEP *Annual Reviews,* from 1976 to 1981, identify issues of major world concern. The issues are all equally important and interact with one another. In this list of major global environmental concerns, we can clearly see the impact of agriculture:

1976: ozone, environmental cancer—soil loss, firewood.

1977: chemicals and the environment, environmental disease—malaria, agro-industrial residues, energy conservation.

1978: chemicals and the environment, environmental disease—malaria, agro-industrial residues, increasing agricultural base for food production, energy conservation.

1979: environmental disease—schistosomiasis, pesticide resistance, noise pollution, tourism and environment.

1980: climatic change—deforestation, carbon dioxide and the carbon cycle; environmental health—heavy metal hazards; transport and the environment; environmental effects of military activity; the child and the environment.

1981: use and management of renewable resources—groundwater; toxic chemicals and the human food chain; environmental economics.

In the next chapters several of these issues will be described in detail: soil loss, energy conservation, increasing the agricultural base for food production, the carbon dioxide issue, and groundwater. But, at this point, we will highlight three of the issues that UNEP has brought to the attention of the nations: ozone, soil loss, and chemicals in the environment. These issues illustrate the magnitude of stress now felt on the "normative design" of the planet and reveal the need for change, particularly in the technologies of our agriculture.

Atmospheric ozone

The ozone shield is vital for our survival. Ozone represents one-millionth of one part of our atmosphere. Most of it is concentrated in the stratosphere, from 10 to 50 kilometers in altitude, with high concentrations at the 30-kilometer level. Although slight in density, it is crucial for protecting the fragile balances of life on the surface of the earth. Ozone depletion is caused by aerosol propellants and refrigerants, stratospheric aviation, nitrogen oxide gases from surface exhausts, the oxidation of inorganic nitrogenous fertilizers, and increased use of nitrogen-fixing legumenous plants. These oxides of nitrates and carbons combine with pure oxygen and thus cause a reduction of the concentration of ozone (O_3).

The Royal Swedish Academy of Sciences states that the "man-made" contribution to the amount of nitrogen annually fixed was, a few years ago, about 25%. This has now risen to nearly 50%, because of the huge demand for nitrogen fertilizer and the increased use of fossil fuel.[7] Humanity produces as much nitrogen as the terrestrial and aquatic system: 120 million metric tons. Our atmosphere has an enormous concentration of nitrogen compounds, but like almost everything else in the ecosystem, all are finely balanced. Today, we release as much nitrogen as nature. This is part of the reason for alarm.

On a global scale, we must be concerned about the extent to which human activities have increased the emission of nitrous oxide into the atmosphere, some of which reaches the stratosphere where it plays an important role in regulating the earth's ozone shield against ultraviolet radiation. The Swedish Academy estimates that an increase of 1% in the emission rate of nitrous oxide will cause a 0.2% decrease in stratospheric ozone, influencing the penetration of ultraviolet light.[8] Nitrogen fixation by the fertilizer industry amounted to 26% of terrestrial fixation. On the basis of present trends this will increase to equal natural biological fixation by 1989.[9]

The World Meterological Organization (WMO) of the United Nations is establishing a "Global Environmental Monitoring System" (GEMS) with the hope of establishing 20 stations to monitor atmospheric pollution. About half of these stations are now in place. At this time, the main concern of this effort is to monitor chemical composition and changes in oxides of nitrogen, fluorohydrocarbons, and carbon dioxide, along with atmospheric particulate pollutants.[10]

As one of the Food and Agricultural Organization reports states:

> Very little is known about the oxidization of nitrates from soils by denitrification. Most measurements suggest 30% loss of all nitrogen into the air. The subject of denitrification taking place in the field, particularly under conditions of high nitrogen fertilizer use, is in urgent need for more intensive research.[11]

A report of the American Chemical Society states:

> Although most oxides of nitrogen are found in the low level of the troposphere, the conclusion for the entire subject is that man-made contributions to the entire biosphere (from ocean depths to the limits of the stratosphere) are of primary importance.[12]

The British Department of the Environment reached similar conclusions:

> The depletion of the ozone layer has possible ultimate adverse

consequences for human health and beyond. There is a need to take action . . . but it can only be done on an international basis. It will take time to be better informed; but, in the meantime, prudence demands that attempts should be made to seek alternatives which meet the needs of the public and of industry, but which do not pose the same potential threat to the stratosphere.[13]

Will the increasing pollution of the atmosphere change the course of atmospheric evolution? Will earth become as inhospitable as Venus? What is the impact of atmospheric chemical change on climate? It is hard to find answers to these questions, and at this time we can only make informed guesses.

The oxidization of inorganic nitrogen fertilizers and, perhaps in time, the increase in oxidization of nitrogen-fixing legumes from expanded planting may have adverse effects on the ozone shield. The heavy use of inorganic fertilizers and their impact upon the ozone shield must be considered when we ask about food for tomorrow.

Soil loss and firewood utilization

The world's food-producing system is steadily losing vast areas of productive land. It has been estimated that against the 1.5 billion hectares of land (1 hectare = approx. 2.47 acres) currently used for crop production, nearly 2 billion hectares have been lost in historic times. If present trends in soil loss continue, all the programs for adding more land to the food production system may not compensate for the area lost as a result of soil degradation and through competing land use.[14] A land area the size of Luxembourg (200,000 to 300,000 hectares) is lost annually to desertification. This does not include decline in fertility or land lost to salinity or alkalinity.

The area of cultivated land per person may be halved by the year 2000. The United Nations report of the World Conference on Desertification, held in Nairobi in 1976, states:

Estimates of present losses give rise to a pessimistic outlook, suggesting that the world will lose close to one-third of its arable lands by the end of the century. Such losses will take place while the food requirements of the human race are rising at least as rapidly as the human population is growing.[15]

Associated with the loss of soil is the question of firewood.[16] The UNEP *Annual Review* of 1977 points out that in the so-called Third World, 95% of all households use firewood as the major source of fuel. In 1974 the Food and Agricultural Organization calculated that 45% of wood timber produced was for firewood and charcoal. South of the Sahara 95% of wood used is for fuel. Of all "Developing World" wood, 86% is cut for fuel. In the "Developing World" wood accounts for 28% of all fuel used.

Throughout the world, forests are threatened. Until 1940 forests had completely disappeared in China. Much of India today experiences forest decline, though massive efforts are under way for reforestation. With the loss of forests, upland watersheds are destroyed, causing lowland flooding and destructive sedimentation of reservoirs and streams. In time, regions become arid, and the desert advances.

Chemicals in the environment

We use about four million chemical substances at home, in industry, in agriculture, and for disease control. About 60,000 chemical compounds are commercially produced. For all purposes, about one million chemicals are produced each year, while at the same time several thousand new chemical substances are developed.

Of particular concern are the unknown aspects of low-exposure rates over 20 to 30 years. When chemicals like antibiotics are fed to livestock, what are the effects on human health?

Of 1000 major chemical pesticides, 225,000 tons are sold annually for agriculture, forestry, food storage, and horticultural and household use. The impact on what are called "non-target" organisms is hardly understood. Chemical residues are everywhere. Algae, resulting from phosphates and nitrates, bloom in our water supplies. Runoff from fertilizer applications is a worldwide problem. Of growing concern is the impact on the atmosphere, lithosphere, biosphere, and hydrosphere of wastes of mercury, cadmium, lead, and gaseous emissions of sulfur oxide, nitrogen oxide, carbon monoxide, carbon dioxide, and the chlorofluoromethanes.

Resistance to pesticides is becoming a sobering concern. In 1965 the Food and Agricultural Organization of the United Nations estimated that 182 resistant strains of insects were attacking our main food crops. By 1977 the number expanded to 364. During 1969, 15 species of mosquitoes had developed resistance to DDT, and by 1976 there were 43 species.

Virtually all global ecosystems are now contaminated with DDT and other chlorinated hydrocarbons. This contamination is found in rainfall, soil, songbirds, ocean fish, desert gazelle, Antarctic penguins, mothers' milk, and infants' bodies from Papua New Guinea to Ghana. The increase in malaria as a consequence of resistance to DDT and other chemicals holds millions of people in sickness. Today malaria is again one of the most widespread environmental diseases of the world.[17]

Because of the increase of the production and use of chemical compounds, humankind has become more and more exposed to the deleterious effects of many of them. Toxic chemicals in food chains cause toxic effects, especially when people are exposed to them over long periods of time.

Toxic chemicals appear in contaminated vegetable parts, residues, ethylene oxides for fumigations, and bread from wheat and cereals treated with alkyl-mercury fumigants. The same can be said about soil contaminants, from toxic chemicals discharged intentionally or accidentally into rivers and lakes from sewage effluent. Many bacterial toxins contaminate our food. There is also the problem of mycotoxins from molds in animal feeds and antibiotics used in the livestock industry and animal products.

While doing research at UNEP in Nairobi in 1981, I noticed a poster announcing the UNEP World Environmental Day. The poster pictured a plate of food sitting on top of the globe with a crop duster flying overhead. The poster stated: "For the general public, food is the major source of exposure to toxic chemicals."

In their book *Food Pollution: The Violation of Inner Ecology*, Gene Marine and Judith Van Allen write:

Every time a natural substance is removed from a food, every time an adulterant is added to a food, the balance in nature is disturbed. The chemical and cellular process within the body cells cannot reach to the passing whims of chemicals without disturbance in function. It took thousands of years for the body to adjust itself to changing environmental conditions. When these conditions are suddenly altered by the actions of men, the cells cannot make the adjustments . . . disease is the result.[18]

The authors point out that when we build dams, cut down forests, plow prairies, or mine, we ask, "What are the environmental consequences?" But we have not yet asked this question about the violation of our inner ecology. They suggest that we are tinkering with virtually everything that goes into our bodies. They ask: "Have you ever thought about what goes into your inner ecology when you have a hot dog and a bottle of beer at the ball park?" Their answer:

Dyes, bleaches, emulsifiers, antioxidants, preservatives, flavors, buffers, noxious sprays, acidifiers, alkalizers, deodorants, moisteners, drying agents, extenders, thickeners, sweeteners, anticaking and foaming agents, fortifiers, monosodium glutamates, sodium nitrates, diethylstilbestrol, butylated hydroxytoluene, etc. . . . a witch's brew of dimensions unknown in the creative broth of the sea. Well over one billion pounds of food additives per year go into U.S. food processing, involving 25,000 additives.[19]

It all adds up to what can be called *chronic toxicity.* Toxic chemicals are within us and around us.

The history of the conquest of the land

Agriculture had its beginnings about 7000 years ago on the fertile alluvial plains of Mesopotamia and the valley of the Nile. The climate was arid. Crops were grown by irrigation, producing excess. Agriculture flourished for centuries until the farmer and the shepherd began their struggle. Between 17 and 25 million people irrigated 21,000 square miles of the 35,000-square-mile alluvium. But, in time, the erosion of the hinterland caused by foresters and herdsmen aggravated the problem of canal silting from the silt-laden waters of the Euphrates River, and not even hordes of captive slaves could keep the canals open. Invasions of nomads from out of the grasslands and desert regions brought about the final collapse.

In similar ways agriculture along the Nile delta failed. The ox and plow were used. Labor could then be spared from farming. It was diverted to the building of pyramids. Soon after, the canals silted, and the whole system collapsed.

Beyond the Jordan is what Moses described as the land flowing with milk and honey. Today, the soil has eroded away. One can see the ruins of the villages near Hebron, which, three millenia ago, were situated on fertile slopes. The glaring hills of Judea, not far from Jerusalem, are now dotted with only a few of their former villages.

About 4500 years ago, a Semitic tribe swept in from the desert and occupied the eastern shore of the Mediterranean and established the cities of Tyre and Sidon. In time the trees in the mountains were cut down, and everything was lost—slopes as well as flooded-out narrow coastal plain. It was from these same mountains that King Solomon made an agreement with the King of Tyre to furnish cypress and cedars for the construction of the Temple at Jerusalem. Solomon supplied 80,000 lumberjacks and 70,000 workers to skid the logs to the sea. The 4000 square miles of forest area were destroyed. Today, only four small groves of the famous cedars of Lebanon remain. Goats saw to it that seedlings would have no chance of survival. This was a tragedy beyond all measure.

In our time, one can see the continued drama on the southern fringes of the Sahel and the midelevation of Latin America. Likewise, the deserts of Syria are the record of the invasion of the Persian armies in A.D. 610-612. The infrastructure of a fragile agriculture was disrupted, and the soil soon disappeared.

For centuries, the forests of China were harvested, but not replanted. For centuries the dikes, made from the eroded soil of the original forest, were used to strengthen and raise the banks of the great rivers in the valleys and plains. But early in this century the battle was finally lost, and millions of low-lying farms were flooded. Famine took its tragic toll. The struggle went on for 4000 years.

The function of forests was finally understood—whether it

be in China, ancient Cyprus, North Africa, or the highlands of Italy and France. This history is similar everywhere. During the ensuing period, unresolved conflict arose between herdsmen, farmers, and foresters. The invasion of armies and population pressures on the land were ruinous. The breakdown of agricultural infrastructures of law, water use, and distribution and soil conservation practices were a part of this history.

The result of all this: the irrevocable loss which equals 50% of the earth's original arable soil deposits. The trend accelerates, particularly in North and South America and Africa.

As early as the 1930s W. C. Lowdermilk observed:

If the soil is destroyed, then our liberty of choice and action is gone, condemning this and future generations to needless privations and dangers. So big is this job . . . of saving our good land from further damage and of reclaiming to some useful purpose vast areas of seriously damaged land . . . that full cooperation of the individual interests of farmers with technical leadership and assistance of the government is not only desirable, but necessary, if we are to succeed.[20]

Lowdermilk stresses one further issue: "Land is not an economic commodity. It is an integral part of the nation, even as its people are, and requires protection by the individual owner and by the nation as well." [21]

In Palestine in 1939 Lowdermilk drafted an "Eleventh Commandment." He wondered if Moses would have been inspired to deliver it along with the original ten if he had been able to foresee what suicidal agriculture would do to the land of the holy earth.

Thou shalt inherit the Holy Earth as a faithful steward, conserving its resources and productivity from generation to generation. Thou shalt safeguard thy fields from soil erosion, thy living waters from drying up, thy forests from desolation, and protect thy hills from overgrazing by thy herds, that thy descendents may have abundance forever. If any shall fail in this stewardship of the land, thy fruitful fields shall become sterile, stony ground and wasting gullies, and thy descendents shall decrease and live in poverty or perish from off the face of the earth.[22]

2 The American Land

U. S. agriculture is in crisis. It is a part of the world food crisis. The two are interrelated. Human demands for food and land resources are high, yet these resources are now severely limited and under heavy stress. World food shortages have resulted in pressure on American farmland for increased food production. This has caused a severe stress upon our own agricultural resource base. Likewise, increased U. S. demand for food and fiber from other nations has resulted in similar patterns of impact.

Population demands

In 1930 the world's population was estimated to be at about two billion. Today it is much more than four billion, and in 20 years it will rise to more than six billion. World population continues to grow at a rate of between 80 and 90 million people each year. Annual food production is increasing in most nations at the rate of 2%. This is below the annual rate of population growth (from 2.5% to nearly 4% in some places).

With existing agricultural resources, we still have the possibility to feed ourselves at the six billion figure, but not much beyond that point. This assumes, of course, that a social will is generated in time to give first priority to overcoming food deficits and improving our technologies and patterns of resource use. We can barely feed ourselves now, and soon our numbers will be increased another 30%. There are limits beyond which we cannot go. In 1983 the World Bank reported that during the past decade per capita average food intake, measured in calories of food energy, declined 11% across the entire continent of Africa.

Of equal importance to population numbers are food and food-related resource demands. During the period when populations are growing by 30%, worldwide soil loss will also be 30%. Beyond this reality of soil loss is the rising demand for fossil fuel and fresh water for food production. It will not be possible for the world to maintain the same quality of diet which prevails in the United States at this time. In fact, if we continue using present technologies of food production, processing, storage, and distribution of the industrialized nations, we will not be able to maintain the present quantity or quality of food supplies.

In addition to the technological side of sustained food production, food supply depends on the ability to purchase food at a price to cover the costs of production and distribution. It depends on the severity of international competition for food. The rich nations will undoubtedly manage. Every year, as a result of increased purchasing power and often unfavorable weather, the demand for food increases substantially in the Soviet Union, China, and Western and Eastern Europe. Although the need for food in most of the food-deficit nations is severe, the majority of the world's excess food will not be moving in these directions unless some radically unexpected breakthroughs take place in the struggle for the development of international food programs. No major movement has taken place since the 1973 United Nations World Food Conference in Rome.[1]

We need to dispel the fallacy that the United States is the world's breadbasket. The United States produces about 13% of the annual world production of principal feed grains and wheat and rice. Of all grain produced in the world (about 1.4 billion metric tons), only one of every eight bushels enters the international market.[2] Most is consumed locally. Of the grain available in the international market, 60% comes from the United States. This 60% portion of the international market represents only 7% of the present worldwide production of grain. Nonetheless, this is substantial. But other nations have their own breadbaskets, too, and they can be improved.

In terms of international food aid (food shipments to food-deficit nations) throughout the 1970s, U. S. food aid averaged about 4% of our total food exports, while 96% of our exported food went into direct sales to the nations that could afford and were willing to buy. It is also important to remember that we import 50% to 60% of our volume of food from all around the world in the forms of beef, mutton, sugar, coffee, tea, fresh vegetables, tropical fruits, cocoa, and fish and animal by-products for stocking our own livestock feed industry.[3] To illustrate this point, the January 21, 1980, edition of *Time* magazine contained the following chart covering our three major grains: [4]

(In millions of metric tons)

Commodity	World Production	U.S. Production	U.S. Exports
Corn	406	193	55
Wheat	403	58	36
Soybean	95	61	22

There will be a 300% increase in food demand by the end of the century.[5] Can this be met? Our farm exports have almost tripled in volume between 1971 and 1981. This has earned us 44.7 billion dollars in needed income to help balance our payments for imported oil. But the problem remains:

> Many agricultural experts worry that the lure of lucrative foreign markets is leading farmers to abuse the land by deep plowing, removal of windbreaks, and excessive pumping from underground water reservoirs . . . the result they fear will be increasingly severe soil erosion that could dramatically prejudice this country's ability to produce food for ourselves and others in the future.[6]

It would be premature to throw up our hands and announce to the world that our country will de-emphasize food exports. It is clear, however, that unless farmers and government can work together to stop erosion and depletion of this country's precious land resources, the wisdom of unlimited planting of crops for export will come into question.[7]

The necessity to cover the costs of fuel imports, in conjunction with the international struggle for some kind of a balance in military deterrent, determines greatly the directions American agriculture will take. The question of the global balance of political and economic power is a formative aspect of American agriculture.

The extent of cropland

Of the total land surface of the contiguous United States (2.26 billion acres), between 344.5 and 540 million acres (almost 40% of the nation's nonfederal land) have a potential for agriculture. The lower acreage figure is based on the 1977 Federal Soil Conservation report of prime land estimates, as well as actual acreage under cultivation. The higher figure (540 million acres) reflects a 1977 Soil Conservation Service inventory of all nonfederal land estimates of potentiality of land that possibly can be converted to agricultural land in the future. Definitions and criteria are important factors behind these discrepancies of estimates of potentiality.[8]

Agricultural land is defined as land currently used to produce agricultural commodities, or lands that have potential for such production. These lands have a favorable combination of soil quality, growing season, moisture supply, size, and accessibility.[9] Agricultural commodities include food, fiber, forage, oilseed, ornamental materials, wood for all purposes, including seed production and planting stock, and potentiality for biomass for energy production.

Prime farmland is the best land for farming. Prime acres are flat or gently rolling and susceptible to little or no soil erosion. They are our most energy-efficient acres, producing the most food, feed, fiber, forage, and oilseed crops with the least amount of fuel, fertilizer, and labor. Prime farmland combines favorable soil qualities, growing seasons, and moisture supply. Under careful management it can be farmed continuously and at a high level of productivity without degrading either the environment or the resource base. Prime farmland includes land that is currently used as cropland, pastureland, rangeland, forestland, and other uses. It does not include land converted to urban development, transportation, or water.[10] Cropland is defined as land that includes row crops, close-grown field crops, hay crops, rotation hay and pasture, nursery crops, orchards, and other similar specialty crops—summer fallow and other cropland not harvested or pastured.

About three million acres of prime farmland (including forest, range, and pastureland) are being lost every year to nonagricultural purposes. Because present existing and potential estimates were made in 1977, more than 15,000,000 acres should be deducted from these total figures. Between now and the year 2000, we will build on as much land as we have done in our national history. We will consume additional land (mostly prime) equivalent to New Hampshire, Vermont, Massachusetts, Rhode Island.[11] Loss of this land reduces the nation's food supply by 20%.[12]

In 1977, the U. S. Soil Conservation Service produced the following information in the form of several maps. The information has been converted into this chart.[13]

Nonfederal Cropland and Total Prime Farmland (Contiguous U.S.A.)

(In millions of acres)

Region	State	Total Potential Prime	In Production	Difference
Pacific	Washington	2.0	1.4	0.6
	Oregon	2.4	1.8	0.6
	California	7.8	6.5	1.3
Mountain	Montana	1.2	0.9	0.3
	Idaho	3.5	3.0	0.5
	Wyoming	0.2	0.2	0.0
	Nevada	0.3	0.2	0.1
	Utah	0.6	0.6	0.0
	Colorado	1.8	1.6	0.2
	Arizona	1.1	1.1	0.0
	New Mexico	0.5	0.5	0.0
Northern Plains	North Dakota	13.9	12.7	1.2
	South Dakota	5.1	4.3	0.8
	Nebraska	14.2	11.9	2.3
	Kansas	27.3	19.5	7.7
Southern Plains	Oklahoma	15.6	8.4	7.2
	Texas	37.5	17.6	19.9
Lake States	Minnesota	19.5	15.3	4.2
	Wisconsin	10.3	6.5	3.8
	Michigan	8.4	5.7	2.7

Corn Belt	Iowa	19.1	16.9	2.2
	Missouri	15.1	9.5	5.6
	Illinois	21.4	19.1	2.3
	Indiana	14.2	11.5	2.7
	Ohio	11.2	9.2	2.0
Delta States	Arkansas	13.3	6.6	6.7
	Louisiana	10.2	5.3	4.9
	Mississippi	9.3	5.2	4.1
Southeast	Alabama	7.8	2.9	4.9
	Georgia	7.8	3.6	4.2
	South Carolina	3.5	1.5	2.0
	Florida	1.4	0.4	1.0
Appalachian	West Virginia	0.5	0.3	0.2
States	Virginia	4.3	1.5	2.8
	Kentucky	6.0	3.3	2.7
	Tennessee	6.4	3.1	3.3
	North Carolina	5.6	2.7	2.9
Northeast	Maine	0.8	0.3	0.5
	Vermont	0.4	0.1	0.3
	New Hampshire	0.1	0.1	0.0
	Massachusetts	0.4	0.2	0.2
	Connecticut	0.4	0.1	0.3
	New York	4.0	2.3	1.7
	Pennsylvania	4.4	2.3	2.1
	Maryland	1.3	0.8	0.5
	New Jersey	1.2	0.5	0.7
	Delaware	0.3	0.3	0.0
Total		344.5	230.0	114.5

The difference between actual cropland under production (230 million acres) and total estimated cropland (574.5 million acres) points to the basis on which estimated potentials were made. States with large differences are revealing. California's expansion depends on increased water and irrigation facilities to desert lands. Nebraska, Kansas, Texas, and Oklahoma might expand to windblown prairie and semiarid lands. Expansion of cropland in Minnesota, Wisconsin, and Michigan means more forest and woodland clearing within the headwaters of the Mississippi River. Expanding production in Iowa, Missouri, and Illinois means going from hill country pastures to annual cropping systems. In Arkansas, expansion assumes trying one's luck on very thin soil. In Alabama, Georgia, Mississippi, and South Carolina, it means clearing more woodlands. The same thing can be assumed for Tennessee, North Carolina, New York, and Pennsylvania.

The higher estimates of the extent of our agricultural potentials are based on figures like these:

The greatest potential for conversion is pasture and native pasture (51.4 million acres), followed by rangeland (38.9 million acres), forestland (30.9 million acres), and other lands which include farmsteads, windbreaks, etc. (3.4 million acres).[14]

How can we think of a stable future for American agriculture without grass-covered, wind-prone, and windblown semiarid rangeland in the Great American Desert, or without pastures, windbreaks, and farmsteads? The report goes on to say that:

Determinations of cropland potential were made by a group representing a variety of USDA agencies. They were made on the basis of 1976 commodity prices as well as development and production costs.[15]

The estimate of potentials refers to the fact that those states having the most land for conversion to cropland are those in the South and Midwest. This was pointed out with reference to converting pasture, native pasture, and rangeland, particularly west of the 100th meridian (except Florida). The Soil Conservation Service estimates that there are about 125 million acres of rural land with a high or medium potential for conversion to cropland.[16]

Thus, the extent of agricultural land and agricultural land potential is from 344.5 to 540 million acres. It is best, for a while at least, to work with this lower figure which represents present realities. It is this lower figure which is directly involved in the feeding of our nation, with 25% to 30% of the total production going overseas for many purposes.

For now, the questions are: What is happening to this land? Is there enough for tomorrow? What is the extent of loss from erosion, salinization, alkanization, acid rain, compaction, and nonagricultural competitive use? What are the potentialities of our water resources and of the condition of the farmer, the farm family, and the rural community? Trends and potentials in the availability of prime agricultural land have to be determined on a wider basis than potential acreage and commodity price prediction.

The extent of cropland loss

The Soil Conservation Service uses a "Land Capability Classification System" to group soils into compatibility classes on the
basis of their susceptibility to erosion. Classification numbers
are from I to VII. In general, Class I lands are considered to
have attributes that can sustain intensive cultivation without
soil damage. Classes I to IV range to the upper limits considered to be safe for annual cultivation, and then only with
extensive conservation treatment at these higher-ranging
classes.

Soil erosion is usually measured or estimated in terms of
tons-per-acre loss per year. Approximately one ton of topsoil
is equivalent to one cubic yard. One inch of topsoil covering
one acre weighs about 165 tons. Six inches of topsoil, covering
one acre, the depth that is normally cultivated in modern agriculture, weighs approximately 1000 tons. Thus, an estimate
that a given field is losing 10 tons per acre per year (and the
U. S. averages range from 9 to 24 tons per acre per year and
in many places, more than twice this rate) means that it will
lose an inch of topsoil every 15 to 20 years and the whole
plow layer in about 100 years.[17] Under exceptional conditions,
rates in excess of 100 tons per acre per year have been recorded in the Northwest, caused by rapid spring snowmelt
when soil that was frozen under the snow thaws.

The Soil Conservation Service considers a loss of 5 tons per
acre per year tolerable. This means that this amount of soil
can be lost "without a serious reduction of future agricultural
productivity." [18] Ideally, the figure should reflect the rate of
new topsoil formation (about one inch every 300 to 1000
years, depending on climatic and vegetative cover conditions).
It is difficult to find any place in the world where soil is being
built up, even though in most places it is quite easy to build
soil with good management. Soil is not only a renewable resource, it is one which can be increased beyond its original
level. But the process has been dangerously reversed almost
everywhere in the world.

U. S. Federal Government soil-loss measurements are only
estimates. The last comprehensive estimate was done in 1977,

and it measured only wind erosion on the 10 Great Plains states, not gully or streambed erosion.

Erosion has always been a part of civilization. In the United States, essays and government reports on erosion date back to the middle of the 17th century, but it was not until the early 1930s that the nation began to get serious about the subject, and then only temporarily. In 1939 the first chief of the U.S. Soil Conservation Service reported:

> In the short life of this century we have essentially destroyed 282,000,000 acres of crop and rangeland. Erosion is destructively active on 775,000,000 additional acres. About 100,000,000 acres of cropland, much of it representing the best cropland that we have, is finished in this country. It cannot be restored. We are losing every day as the result of erosion the equivalent of two hundred 40-acre farms.[19]

Pimentel's group reports that "it is estimated that we have lost one-third of the topsoil from U.S. cropland in use today."[20] Lester Brown notes in *The Worldwide Loss of Cropland:*

> The Council for Agricultural Science and Technology, supported by a consortium of midwestern universities, reported in 1975 that a "third of all U.S. cropland was suffering soil losses too great to be sustained without a gradual but ultimately disastrous decline in productivity."[21]

Our nation has suffered a loss of one-third of its cropland, and another third is seriously threatened at this time. In 1975 the total loss was about three billion tons, the same amount that was blown away during the Dust Bowl of the early 1930s. Today, we are losing at least four billion tons. This is a 25% increase in loss over one of the most tragic chapters in our national history.[22]

According to the National Resource Inventories Report of 1977, nearly one-fourth of all U. S. cropland is eroding in excess of five tons per acre per year. The Government Accounting Office (GAO) did a study on soil loss on 283 randomly selected farms located in the Great Plains, Corn Belt, and Pacific Northwest. Of these farms 84% were losing soil in excess of five tons per acre per year. This kind of loss effectively discounts the future.

This loss of four billion tons per year is equivalent to a freight train of gondola cars, stretching 633,000 miles — a distance that would encircle the globe 24 times or would reach from the earth to the moon, back to the earth, and towards the moon again.[23] As former U. S. Secretary of Agriculture Bob Bergland said:

> We're on a collision course with disaster . . . our water supplies are being reduced, we have whole watersheds where the groundwater is being depleted, and we have mined our soil. In fact, the erosion of America's farmland today is probably at a record rate, and this simply cannot go on.[24]

Despite a significant investment in conservation practices by the federal government and private landowners, *The National Agricultural Lands Study* reports that erosion from American lands continues at a disturbing rate.[25] The report indicates that: "The 1977 National Resource Inventory shows a national 1977 average annual loss from sheet and rill erosion (only) at about 4 billion tons." [26] This does not take into account the massive losses from wind erosion, and acreage of prime farmland lost to salinity and alkalinity, and nonagricultural land conversion. Loss has to be measured in terms beyond tons per acre per year. Soil fertility, level of organic fraction, depth of topsoil, and physical characteristics also have to be taken into consideration.

Until now the tragedy of American cropland loss has been masked by ever-increasing increments of fossil-fuel-based chemical fertilizer and unusually favorable weather patterns of this past century. When fertilizer becomes limited in supply (and costly), and our weather shifts to a more normal pattern (less favorable for crops), these massive soil losses will be felt, perhaps for the first time, in a most significant way. Then the myth of American agriculture and its soil base will be shattered.

What does this add up to in terms of available cropland for tomorrow?

> If erosion in this area [fertile Midwest and Corn Belt] is allowed to continue at the 1977 rate, USDA estimates that

potential corn and soybean yields would probably be reduced by 15 to 30 percent on some soils by the year 2030.[27]

The report continues:

The nation may be losing an equivalent of 1.01 million acres of cropland annually to erosion. This is based on the assumption that six inches of topsoil weighs about 1,000 tons and that the loss of this amount of topsoil is equivalent to an irreversible conversion of an acre of cropland.[28]

Of course, and the report so states, some land could become unproductive long before six inches are lost.

These acre equivalents represent the gradual loss of productivity that may be occurring over millions of acres of American farmland.[29]

If one includes wind erosion (this information is not available outside of the 11 Great Plains states), the figure expands by a minimum of 240,000 acres. Over the next 50 years, up to 62 million acre equivalents could be lost to wind, assuming the 1977 rate of erosion continues at its present and often accelerated rate.[30] *The National Agricultural Lands Study* summarizes soil productivity loss: [31]

Acre-equivalent of soil productivity lost annually from soil erosion on agricultural lands in the United States
(Thousands of Acres)

Agricultural Land Use	Types of Soil Erosion				
	Sheet & Rill	Gully	Stream-bank	Wind	Total Loss
Cropland	1,010	?	?	240	1,250
Pasture	53a	?	?	b	53
Rangeland	94c	?	?	c	94
Forestland	303d	?	?	b	308
Total Acre-Equivalents					1,705

a Source: USDA, 1980, RCA Appraisal, Part I, Table 3B-1.

b Probably negligible.

c Source: USDA, 1980, RCA Appraisal, Part I, Table 3C-2. This includes sheet, rill and wind erosion. Excess erosion over 2 t/a/y (felt by USDA to be the tolerance limit for rangeland) in tons, divided by 500 = acre-equivalents of loss. Rangeland, because of arid climates and thin topsoils, is more rapidly damaged by soil erosion, thus the use of only a 3-inch topsoil loss to approximate loss of productivity.

d Source: USDA, 1980 RCA Appraisal, Part I, Table 3D-5. Erosion over 5 t/a/y was found in the NRI only on grazed forestlands in Capability Classes IV, VII, and VIII.

The annual total of a 1.7 million acre equivalent loss is alarming, particularly in view of the fact that this figure is partial and does not take into account other major categories of soil loss. The implications of this loss are difficult to estimate in terms of constraint on the future of U. S. agriculture. As demands on U.S. agriculture grow, and a consequent expansion onto land classes beyond IV (more arid prairie and desert lands and into forests and woodlands) occurs, rates of soil loss from erosion will likely skyrocket—far beyond the 25% increase since the days of the Dust Bowl.

The following statistics sum up the magnitude of soil loss in the United States:

The United States will lose 26 square miles of its land today. It will lose another 26 square miles tomorrow, and every day this year. But not to a foreign power. We are giving up our land to the ravenous demands of an unrealistic food system.

In 1980, and again in 1981, three million acres of farmlands will be lost to erosion. Five billion tons of topsoil are displaced annually, enough to cover all five boroughs of New York City with a 13½ foot deep layer of soil.

Man-made blights, these. Symptoms of a food system that is dangerously out of touch with our new world of limited resources.[32]

We are working with a cropland base today of between 244 and 450 million acres (after the one-third loss so far suffered). From sheet, rill, and wind erosion alone, the nation is losing close to two million acre equivalents per year. If this rate continues, our soil will be gone (like the Mediterranean steppe, or parts of Sahelian Africa) in 150 to 225 years. This is a tragic prediction.

Cropland loss to salinization and alkalinization

A major historical problem of irrigated agriculture the world over is related to the buildup of soluble salts in the soil surface.

This process is called *salinization* and *alkalinization*. The accumulation of the cations of calcium, magnesium, and sodium and the anions of sulfate, chloride, and bicarbonate is called salinization. When these dissolved salts form soda, they become highly alkaline compounds, posing difficult soil problems, involving the development of impermeable and sterile soil on which very little, if anything, can be grown.

Of the 58 million acres of irrigated land in the United States, between 150,000 and 200,000 acreas of semiarid uplands are under the threat of salinization and alkalinization. This means that more than 20% of Western soils have significant salinity and alkalinity problems, because most of these lands were at one time ancient salt-water seabeds. These soils can be found from Montana and the Dakotas to parts of Texas, New Mexico, Arizona, California, Colorado, Utah, and Nevada. Dry cropland areas where yields have been significantly reduced or eliminated are estimated to range from 150,000 to 200,000 acres. The number of these acres is increasing annually at the rate of about 10%.[33]

Irrigated crops on the 58 million acres are large consumers of water. So also are the living plants that extract the water from the salt-laden soil. They leave salts in the upper profile of the soil, which results in a further concentration of dissolved mineral salts.

Throughout my own lifetime, in my home state of California, I have observed the problem of salinization, alkalinization, and water-logging. In the expanding west side of the Central San Joaquin Valley, the Central California Project annually brings five million acre-feet of water to the westlands. Along with it come two million tons of salt accumulation. This is enough salt to cover 1800 acres of land one foot deep. It will take about $11 billion (1980) and 100 years of work to complete a network of nearly 300 miles of drainage canals, salt marshes, and evaporation reservoirs to control the problem, which, in 100 years, will involve the removal of more than three million tons of salt annually. Some 400,000 acres are presently enduring stress. Soon, a million acres will be seriously threatened.[34]

The Environmental Protection Agency (EPA) has attempted to estimate the total costs of salt control for the lower

Colorado basin and Southern California, where "salinity concentrations are now approaching critical levels." [35] By the year 2000, the Colorado River Basin Salinity Control Project, near Yuma, Arizona, will be pumping 2.8 million tons of salt and agrichemical residues into the Sea of Cortez. [36]

One hopeful sign is the research Professor Emanuel Epstein of the University of California at Davis conducted on the sand dunes at the Bodega Bay Marine Laboratory, 50 miles north of San Francisco. The purpose of the research is to breed salt-resistant plants "for discovering a possible solution to one of our oldest farming problems . . . the slow but deadly buildup of poisonous salts in the earth." [37] Positive results would help 4.6 million acres of California's soils affected by salinity. Professor Epstein observes that, at present, about one-third of the world's total irrigated land is affected, a problem that has plagued irrigated land since people began to use the water of the Tigris and Euphrates Rivers for irrigating the land of Mesopotamia, the Fertile Crescent. The University of California team is working with wheat, barley, and tomatoes. They note the rising costs of pumping the limited supplies of fresh water, and the inadequate drainage systems for carrying away leeched saline effluent. One alternative is the development of more salt-tolerant crops. "At least this will extend the time period farmers will have before they have to reclaim the land." [38]

A discussion of this subject in *The National Agricultural Lands Study* concludes:

> Increasing salinity will definitely play a major role in impairing future productivity of cropland in the western states. It appears that management techniques could be employed successfully to minimize this loss, but those techniques will increase crop production costs and may result in much irrigated land becoming less economically competitive, particularly for lower value crops. [39]

Success in salt management assumes there will be: 1) an abundant supply of quality water for leeching purposes; 2) breakthroughs in the genetic development of more salt-tolerant plants; 3) a massive development of more adequate drainage systems; 4) a suitable place to dispose of effluent; 5) and an alternative cropping and livestock system on the drylands. All of these assumptions are difficult to deal with at this time.

Within this problem is the question of the future productivity (and costs of production) of 58 million acres of irrigated land and upwards to 200,000 acres of uplands, presently in summer-fallow crop-rotation schemes.

Soil compaction

In recent years most agricultural areas have experienced a trend toward larger and more capital-intensive farming. As a natural consequence, farm equipment has become larger and heavier. Row cropping has increased by 27%, and rotation with hay crops and pastures has declined 40%. For example, total corn and soybean acreage has increased sharply in Iowa, Wisconsin, and Minnesota since 1965, and hay has dropped proportionally.[40] W. B. Voorhees, in "Soil Tilth Deterioration Under Row Cropping in the Northern Corn Belt: Influence of Tillage and Wheel Traffic," displays data compiled by the Soil Conservation Service of Des Moines, showing the expansion in tillage from 1968 at 443,900 acres, to 9,067,000 acres in 1977.[41] This magnitude of transition is accompanied by an increased use in heavy farm equipment, which causes serious compaction problems. Voorhees concludes his penetrating report:

> Regardless, the relatively good soil tilth enjoyed by farmers in the region should not be taken for granted. Once soil is compacted, it may be more difficult to restore than previously thought. This is especially so for soil compaction below normal tillage depth.[42]

Compaction varies according to soil types, climate variation, farm management practices, and cropping systems. Wet soils and soils lacking significant levels of organic matter are, of course, highly susceptible to compaction. Compaction reduces water and air infiltration, with a consequent high rate of water runoff. It reduces root growth capacity and the availability of plant nutrients. Recovery from freezing conditions is slower. Estimates of yield reduction from compaction are few and, where they have been made, are only in local settings. While rotation and tillage methods can be employed to minimize adverse effects of compaction in the surface horizons, the problem becomes more severe at lower levels of the soil. If the trend in large-scale farming continues, and more is done in row crops and less with livestock and livestock-related farming (pastures, rangelands, hay crops, etc.), the issue of compaction may likely arise as another important constraint in U. S. agriculture.

Competing uses for the land

For many years, about one million acres of good farmland have been converted to nonagricultural purposes each year. This rate has now climbed significantly. The United States is converting its croplands (much of it prime farmland) at the rate of about 12 square miles per day. This represents the equivalent every year of a swath of prime land one-half mile wide, reaching from San Francisco to New York City.[43] Most of these lands are being used for urban and industrial sprawl and highway development, including 40-acre cloverleafs at major intersections. The Federal Reserve Bank of Chicago notes that more than 40% of the housing constructed during the 1970s was built on agricultural land. New commerce, industry, and support facilities accompanying urban sprawl have eaten up more land. More than 90 federal programs that promote economic development, housing, environmental protection, or natural resource development have encouraged the conversion of agricultural land.[44]

New pressures have the potential of making even this present situation insignificant. These new pressures come from the need for alternative energy sources, such as coal and ethanol, and land for the expansion of power transmission lines, hydroelectric facilities, synthetic fuel plants, and accompanying boomtowns associated with all of these new thrusts in energy-resource development.

Until recently, the early effects which energy policy discussions have made on U. S. agriculture have not received careful attention by energy planners. Even to this day, the national mood seems to be willing to trade off environmental stability and a secure food production base in order to maintain an ever-increasing energy-consumption pattern.

As of 1982 the United States was consuming more than 100 billion gallons of gasoline every year. During his term of office President Carter suggested that to offset this figure and to reduce expenditures for foreign oil, we ought to achieve a beginning production of 500 million gallons of ethanol (only 1/20th of our gasoline needs) from crops and crop residues. However, the question is: what is the likely effect of this policy on the agricultural land base? Even though no one really knows, the question needs to be raised.

The Department of Energy (DOE), in a more modest mood, projected the one possibility of producing upwards to 4.7 billion gallons of ethanol by "bringing into production all existing grain land and by supplementing food processing wastes with sugar surplus and fermentable municipal wastes." [45] The DOE report does admit that:

> Achieving this limit would be expensive and would reduce the flexibility of U.S. agricultural land and restrict options for food production.[46]

Basing its calculations on a USDA estimate that United States agriculture produces one billion tons of dry crop and forest residues, the DOE suggests that the U. S. could therefore produce about 54 billion gallons of ethanol per year. But the DOE does not consider the need for the incorporation of this material back into the soil in the attempt to stabilize the organic fraction which now is reduced 40% over its original state.

The modest Carter recommendation of 500 million gallons of ethanol would require about 2.5% of the 1979 United States corn crop—not counting soil loss and energy expenditures for farm power, petrochemicals, and processing—giving, according to some authorities, a negative net result. In terms of acreage requirements to meet this very modest target, 1.8 million acres would have to be used for the production of feedstock for the distilleries.[17] But if a mixture of one part ethanol and nine parts gasoline were used to power America's existing automobile fleet, about 38 million equivalent acres of corn would have to be used for that purpose.

In addition, no one is talking about the impact ethanol production has on land quality with reference to soil erosion, soil fertility, or soil structure.

If surface mining for coal is developed along the lines of the modest DOE energy plan to put this nation into an energy-independent status, about 10 million acres of present grain and rangeland would have to be set aside for mines, stockpiling, haul roads, and related needs. About 25% of this acreage is classified as prime agricultural land.[48] Estimates of land needs for energy development over the next 50 years in the Northern Great Plains alone (including Montana, North and South Dakota, and Wyoming) range from a low of 240,000 acres to a high of 1,473,000 acres by the year 2030.[49] Although much is said about reclamation of farmland following mining operations, there is very little evidence at this time that the disturbed land can be brought back to a full productive state.[50] Whether it is due to coal mining and coal-fired generating plants or ethanol distilleries, the DOE estimates there will be 31 to 41 counties in the United States which will experience boomtown growth conditions and subsequent effects on land, water, air resources, and social services.[51]

Power plants and transmission lines will require an additional use of a great deal of agricultural land. In 1981 the Federal Energy Regulatory Commission estimated a need for about seven million acres (an area the size of Connecticut) of right-of-way to meet production projections for 1990.[52] To keep pace with growing demands for energy, more dams and lakes need to be built. At present, it is estimated that about 10 million acres are used for hydroelectric facilities. The DOE has identified an additional 500 sites that can be developed for such purposes. Both acreage and water issues are involved and have their impact on the agricultural land base. No estimates of total acreage needs are projected.

It is impossible to identify the potential impact of these competitive uses of U. S. farmland. The acreage in question is in the tens of millions, be it for continued urban and industrial sprawl, ethanol production, hydroelectric facilities and power transmission lines, or strip or pit mining. Always, the question of net gain in energy inputs and outputs has to be calculated. So must be measured the trade-offs on soil quality, acid rain, carbon dioxide buildup, and the constant emission of heat into the whole biosphere. However, given a specific focus on the issue of the acreage base of farmlands, W. Wendell Fletcher, vice-president of the American Land Forum of Washington, D. C., states in the conclusion of his report on "Farm Land and Energy: Conflicts in the Making":

> Development pressures in rural areas, the crucial role of agriculture commodities to the U.S. balance of trade, and a rapidly evolving energy technology make the energy-farmland interrelationships a slippery policy conundrum.[53]

Genetic truncation

Plant-breeding programs have played a significant role in setting production records through the genetic improvement of our major crops, but with mixed results. As Wes Jackson puts it, "Success is tied to a time-bomb by a short fuse." [54] Of some 350,000 plant species, about 200 to 300 are readily edible in their present form by the general population. Yet, given this small fraction of the potential, we have come to depend greatly on only 12 or so. It has been through the emphasis on these few plant species that we have come to such a level of monocultural specialization that our security in plant diversity has become highly threatened.

The corn blight of the early 1970s was our early warning. Our short-run gains in high yields have come at the expense of increased vulnerability through a narrowing of the genetic base of many of our crops. We know that resistance to a particular pathogen requires genes that dictate a certain immunological defense mechanism to keep the disease under control. The same holds true for resistance to insects and drought.

During the past 30 years we have manipulated the genetic design of plants to be highly responsive to chemical fertilizers, and in most cases, an abundance of water. With a very firm control on patent rights, seed companies today are part of our fossil-fuel based agriculture. Plant breeders have ignored many genes for disease resistance, preferring those that give high yields in combination with abundant soil fertility and water. Consequently, our genetic base has been seriously narrowed. This is what is meant by the term "genetic truncation." [55] The so-called "improved varieties" of wheat and corn have driven many of the old, local, reliable varieties out of the fields, sometimes to the point of extinction. In many cases, the genetic resource base on which new high-yielding varieties were built has disappeared.

One of the most helpful studies of this problem is presented by Norman Myers in *The Sinking Ark*.[56] In the preface he establishes a broad perspective from which to appreciate the critical trend in genetic truncation.

> This book looks at the prospect for all species on earth, 5-10 million of them. It proposes that we stand to lose at least one million by the end of the century, and several more million within just a few decades. Right now we could be losing one species per day.

> This means not only that our children will live in a world made poorer through the elimination of myriad life forms that have shared the common earth home with humankind, it also means that basic processes of evolution are being altered more drastically than since the sudden disappearance of the dinosaurs, 60 million years ago, and possibly more than since the emergence of life's diversity 3½ billion years ago. And it is all happening within the twinkling of an evolutionary eye.[57]

A concentrated international effort is under way to regain the biological base of the past and to correct the kinds of negative consequences that have emerged during the early days of the so-called Green Revolution. The maintenance of defense mechanisms in plants (as well as animals) requires energy. Genetic structure and solar energy have been replaced with fossil-fuel energy and pesticides. Genetic specialization breaks up our defense, which in the past was from variety. Our options have been seriously reduced. In the process, we have lost a tremendous gene pool, because many plant species and varieties have become extinct following the vast plantings of our few commercially developed coarse and fine grains in most of the agriculture of most of the nation. In the desperate struggle and massive international response for food, food-deficit nations adopted American agricultural technologies, but at the expense of reliable varieties of plants that yield less and were not dependent on fossil-fuel resources and massive quantities of water. Genetic truncation is a further serious constraint to be considered when pondering the question, "Will there be food for tomorrow?"

Another tragic by-product of the rise of energy-intensive agriculture is the fate of natural seed stands, which were widely used only a few decades ago. Since the advent of hybrid seeds, the older seeds have in many cases been lost through neglect, ending a genetic continuity of many millennia. Agricultural researchers are experiencing great difficulty in acquiring stocks of native seeds for preservation programs.[58] The director of the Fort Collins National Seed Storage Facility, Dr. Louis Boss, fears that without sufficient funding, the seed storage program will not be adequate to meet the challenge of genetic erosion. If this challenge is not met, "The consequences of the loss of native seed germplasma are staggering, when one thinks that within one short generation, human beings could throw away key evolutionary links in the food system, all in the name of progress." [59]

Genetic development in the high-yielding varieties, in combination with fossil-fuel based fertilizers and pesticides, has increased yields by more than 50% and in some cases by 300% to 400%. But for how long, and at what ultimate price?

3 Clean Air and Water

Clean air and water are essential for our survival. Like ourselves, agriculture is totally dependent on these resources.

Cropland loss to acid rain

The United States annually discharges about 150 million metric tons of sulfur and nitrogen oxides into the atmosphere as a result of burning massive quantities of fossil fuels such as coal and oil.[1] Through a series of complex chemical reactions these pollutants are converted into photochemical smog and acids and return to the surface of the earth as components of rain or snow. This "acid rain" is having severe impact downwind of the industrial centers all over the world. Although the problem has been identified long ago in Scandinavia (downwind of the Ruhr Valley of Germany), only recently has it become an acute problem in the United States. More than 90 lakes in the Adirondack Mountains of New York State are fishless because of the acidic condition that inhibits reproduction. Recent data indicates that other areas of the United States, such as northern Minnesota and Wisconsin, are vulnerable.[2]

Preliminary research indicates that crop yields can be reduced as a result of both the direct effect of acids on foliage and indirect effects resulting from increased leeching of minerals from soils. Forest productivity is also lessened. A National Research Council project committee reported in the study, *Agricultural Production Efficiency*, that "air pollution is an unwitting constraint on agricultural production efficiency." [3] Evidence of this can be found throughout affected areas in the United States.

The Zinfandel wine producers in California have had to abandon some of their acreage because of pollutants. Some cigar-tobacco producers in the Connecticut Valley have abandoned production. Spinach is disappearing from vegetable farms near many of our cities. Yields of potatoes in the Connecticut Valley have been decreasing since 1960.[4] In my home area of Southern California, I have observed since early childhood the buildup of smog and its resultant damage on citrus groves and the forest trees of the San Bernardino National Forest, located more than 50 miles away. Fluoride and surfur oxides, released into the air by phosphate fertilizer processing in Florida, have blighted numerous citrus orchards.[5] In New Jersey, pollution injury to vegetation has been observed in every county, and damage has been reported to at least 36 commercial crops. Laboratory studies in Southern California found sizeable reductions when measuring yields of crops grown in polluted air in comparison to filtered clean air. Alfalfa yields declined 38%.[6]

By 1974 acid rain covered part of all of the states in the United States east of the 100th meridian, as well as large areas of the West, particularly around Los Angeles, Oregon's Willamette Valley, Tucson, Grand Forks, Nebraska, and New Mexico.[7]

No system of analysis has been developed to measure acre-equivalent losses from acid rain, as has been done in the case of soil erosion. But, given the growing body of evidence, the time may soon come that this kind of general measurement can be made. This will be of particular importance, because the nation will undoubtedly use more and more fossil-fuel energy in the form of coal and synfuels in the forthcoming decades, while at the same time experiencing a relaxation of environmental controls. Coping with the trade-offs of food and fuel is becoming progressively difficult.

Water scarcity

United States agriculture is the major consumer of fresh water. Between 80% and 85% of it is used by agriculture for irrigation alone. This does not take into consideration the processing of our agricultural products.[8] In many regions of the United States, more water is consumed than is available from annual surface flow. This is possible because of the ground-water resources that are now used in our agricultural activities. On a national average, fresh water discharge now exceeds recharge by about one-third.[9]

The key perspective to keep in mind is that the nation's natural water supply has always been out of balance. The Northwest and Northeast have tremendous surplus, while the Southwest and Midwest regions are nearly arid and dependent on a few major rivers for irrigation systems and the major aquifers of the Great Plains.

Groundwater resources have been estimated to have a volume far greater than all surface water and more than the total capacity of all the nation's lakes and reservoirs (including the Great Lakes). The volume is equivalent to about 35 years of surface runoff (100-180 billion acre feet). Yet, increasingly, local demands for irrigation cause mounting stress on these resources.[10] The figure below illustrates this reality.

Groundwater is overdrafted. In the Great Plains 70% of the surface water is depleted rather than being diverted to the normal recharge of the aquifer. Artesian pressure, declining spring and streamflow, land subsidence, and saltwater intrusion problems are strong evidence of the excessive use of our water supply. Indeed, the candle is burning rapidly at both ends.

Most of the vast underground resources deposited over thousands of years have been seriously depleted in a few decades.[11] About 25% of the water used in the United States for all purposes (agriculture, industry, urban living) is pumped from underground aquifers. Between 1950 and 1980 the pumping of these reserves has doubled. Daily 21 billion gallons more water are used than recharged.

The foremost illustration of this reality and its consequences

Overdraft of Groundwater

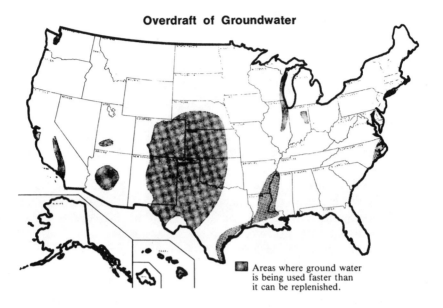

Areas where ground water is being used faster than it can be replenished.

Surface Water Supply

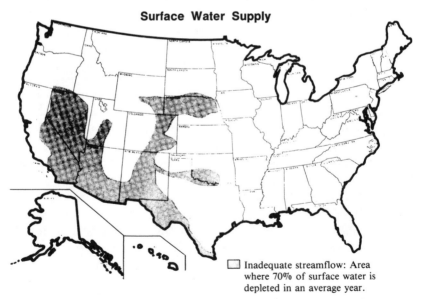

Inadequate streamflow: Area where 70% of surface water is depleted in an average year.

From *The National Agricultural Lands Study*, Interim Report Number Four, "Soil Degradation: Effects on Agricultural Productivity," as prepared by the National Association of Conservation Districts, Washington, D.C., November, 1980, p. 35.

is the massive Ogallala aquifer that stretches from west Texas to northern Nebraska and beyond. Its estimated original water deposit of two billion acre feet is being used up as wantonly as the oil that lies beneath it. Some authorities estimate that as early as the year 2000, water supplies in parts of Nebraska will be so depleted that farming may never return.[12] At the most, the Ogallala aquifer will support pivotal irrigation agriculture for the next 35 to 40 years. It is presently being discharged at a rate of four feet per year. This must be seen in comparison to its recharge rate from rainfall and sparse runoff from the eastern slopes of the Rockies, which is at a rate of one-quarter inch per year.

Already, the trans-Pecos area of Texas is experiencing depleted supplies of water. Large acreages of irrigated croplands have been abandoned and converted to rangeland. Nearly 10 million of a total of 50 million acres of irrigated land in west Texas and eastern New Mexico are threatened.[13]

In his book *From the High Plains,* John Fisher traced the exploitive history of his homeland, the Panhandle of Texas.[14] It began 15 centuries ago when the Alibates quarried flint in the area. Then, for more than a thousand years after the flint was depleted, the land was unoccupied by humans. Three hundred years ago the Indians obtained horses from the Spaniards and were able, mainly with help from the white hide-hunters, to hunt to extinction the buffalo herds. Then came the cattlemen who, by the end of the 1800s, had overgrazed the grasslands. After the First World War, the wheat farmers wore out the soil, and the dust storms of the early 1930s blew away the soil altogether. But then came the oil and gas boom. Petroleum geologists have scrutinized every acre quite thoroughly, and before long, oil—like soil, buffalo, and flint—will be gone.

But this still is not the end of the story of the Texas Panhandle, according to John Fisher. Now water is being exhausted. In 1911, a farmer broke into the Ogallala aquifer, a lens-shaped bed of gravel up to 300 feet thick that extends from Nebraska to north Texas. For millions of years it had accumulated water from rain and runoff from the Rockies. Until World War II, this reservoir was not really used. But today, more water is pumped from it than flows down the entire Colorado River system. About six million acres in Texas alone are being irrigated for the production of fodder for the feedlots of the region. Now, a whole complex of cattle-feeding and beef-packing plants depends on the Ogallala. Over half of the total aquifer was exhausted by 1977, and virtually the rest will be gone within the next 30 to 50 years.[15] Fisher ends this story about his homeland with the following projection of its future:

> Some grains and cotton will still be dry farmed, as they were in my boyhood, but the acreage will be much reduced, and much less lucrative than it is now. For the rule of thumb is that without irrigation, Panhandle land will produce good crops about a third of the time, barely harvestable crops about a third of the time, and nothing at all in the other years.[16]

The National Agricultural Lands Study concludes that in this region the conversion of irrigated lands to dryland production obviously will yield less food and fiber. However, the potential loss has not been estimated. The pumping of groundwater at rates exceeding natural recharge requires that alternative water resources or less demanding crops be employed, or that the land must be eventually phased out of irrigated agriculture. In some areas, because of rising pumping costs, declining water tables will cause abandonment of activities before the water is totally consumed.[17]

The real and lasting cost of this rate of consumption is beyond measure. In terms of geological structure, one has to consider the cost of the great landscape slump in the Phoenix-Tucson corridor, in sections of the San Joaquin Valley of Central California, the sinking landscape around Houston, and the seeping of seawater into freshwater aquifers near many of the nation's coastal cities. No one is able to estimate the costs in water-resource loss from the breakup of water-bearing strata from strip mining, nor from the spoilage of water from nitrate and phosphate buildup from agriculture, let alone from industrial and urban pollutants.

Most Americans are aware that water is disappearing from the Owens Valley in California as it is drained from the eastern slopes of the Sierras to keep the expansion of Los Angeles alive. The battle continues in full heat over the development of the Peripheral Canal to bring Sacramento River water to Southern California. This proposal is to compensate for the diversion of Colorado River water to the Central Arizona Project and to alleviate the impact of diverted water from the north on the encroachment of San Francisco Bay waters into the rich delta region. What will be the impact on agriculture on the Northern Plains if more of the Snake and Yellowstone waters are used for coal-fired steam-generation electrical plants, or for the development of shale oil, which requires about four barrels of water for every barrel of oil produced—about 100,000 acre feet?

Farmers are realizing only too painfully that they can no longer use up to 85% of these precious waters. The competition is great. The trade-offs are expensive. If urban and industrial expansion continues at present rates, and the existing plans for the development of coal-fired steam-generation electrical power stations are partially met, then a great deal of agricultural land in the West will have to be retired by the year 2000.[18]

How much water is needed in the Northern Plains to bring into production the targets set in the Nixon-Ford Project Independence proposal which involves the construction and operation of forty-two 500 to 10,000 megawatt generation plants? Together, they would be generating more than 200,000 megawatts of power to meet projected national energy demands for electrical power by the end of this century.[19] The potential impact on surface and underground water resources is as incalculable and incomprehensible as the impact of this kind of activity on the atmosphere in the form of acid rain, the buildup of carbon dioxide, and loss of farmland. It is also impossible to predict the impact of this plan on U.S. food-production trends.

A warning is already before us. It is alarming to realize, for example, that the University of Arizona in Tucson is studying the economic potential of tumbleweeds. This desert plant in its shredded and pressed form makes good firewood fuel. This is good in one sense, but tragic in another. It is ultimately a sad irony, because not long ago this same university was researching in the field of food production on the surface of "blooming deserts." Now, faced with a food and fiber crop industry threatened by urban and industrial demands for new and old water supplies, the university is directing its efforts to other projects, like using weeds for fuel.

Wes Jackson warns that the water problem may be 10 years down the road. As with energy, much of our food-producing system has been based on very low water costs. Consequently, we have dammed our rivers and salted our valleys. We have tapped our aquifers and have built our economics around cheap water.[20] One day we will have to change the way we use our scarce water supply in the organization of our agriculture.

Carbon dioxide buildup and atmospheric transparency

Carbon dioxide (CO_2) is critical for sustaining life. It is odorless, tasteless, and invisible. But enormous amounts of CO_2 currently are being released into the atmosphere and placed into circulation as a result of incredible rates of fossil-fuel burning for transport, industry, deforestation, and agriculture. This may constitute an insidious pollutant. Many scientists now predict disastrous effects on our climate (and on agriculture) if CO_2 emissions continue to increase at projected rates.[21]

Gus Speth, chairperson of the U.S. Council on Environmental Quality from 1977 to 1981, described the current buildup of CO_2 in the atmosphere as the ultimate environmental dilemma. In February 1981, The International Energy Agency and the Organization for Economic Cooperation and Development (OECD) met in Paris to hold a joint workshop on carbon dioxide research and development. The U.S. Department of Energy is in the early stages of a major 10-year program of research into all aspects of the problem.

Carbon dioxide allows sunlight into the atmosphere, but prevents heat from escaping. The result of the buildup of CO_2 is a gradual increase in the earth's temperature, which can have profound consequences. This is called the "greenhouse effect." One climatologist estimates that by the year 2040, temperatures could be warmer than at any time during the past 125,000 years.[22]

This is said squarely in the face of other evidence that we

have lived through the past 200 years of the most favorable climate within the last 1000 years and that a cooling trend is long overdue. If a warming trend does occur as a result of emissions of CO_2 from massive amounts of fossil-fuel energy, the change needs to be seen in geological perspectives as happening with "lightning quickness." [23] This view is not exaggerated, but represents a consensus of scientific opinion.

Carbon dioxide is not in itself harmful. It is found naturally in the atmosphere. By volume, it constitutes about 0.03% of the air we breathe, compared with about 78% nitrogen and 21% oxygen. We exhale CO_2. Plants and trees absorb CO_2 during the process of photosynthesis in which CO_2 and water are combined in the presence of chlorophyll and sunlight for the manufacture of carbohydrates.[24] All life depends on this small percentage of CO_2 in the fragilely balanced atmosphere.

In fossil fuels (coal, oil, natural gas), CO_2 has been locked up for eons. When fossil fuels are burned, the CO_2 is released. Today, the air we breathe (the protective canopy of our existence) holds about 15% more CO_2 than it did 100 years ago. Population-growth demands are exponential. Consequently, the National Academy of Sciences is predicting that by the end of the 22nd century, atmospheric concentrations of CO_2 may be four to eight times the present rate. This degree of buildup is far beyond tolerances. For example, by early in the 21st century (given present combustion rates), the earth could warm up by 1.8° F. Within 100 years, warming could increase on the order of 11° F.[25]

Carbon dioxide concentrations have been growing since about 1850, when the Industrial Revolution was fueled with a newly developed energy source—coal. The CO_2 level in the Pre-Industrial Revolution atmosphere was 270 to 305 parts per million (ppm).[26] In 1958, it was 311 to 312 ppm. Today it is in the range of 335 to 400 ppm— an increase of 7% since 1958. The level of CO_2 in the atmosphere is predicated to be 380 to 400 ppm by the year 2000. Swedish and Australian scientists have measured the level of CO_2 at Mauna Loa, the South Pole, American Samoa, and Barrow, Alaska. Based on their measurements of what was burned in the form of wood, coal, and oil from 1860 to 1977 and what is scheduled to be burned in oil, gas, coal, and from deforestation between now and the year 2000, the figure of a 15% buildup from the beginning of the Industrial Revolution can be made with a high degree of probability. Paul J. Weitz, commander of the first flight of the Challenger, said at a news conference at the Houston Space Center on April 21, 1983:

> It was appalling to me to see how dirty our atmosphere is getting. Unfortunately, this world is rapidly becoming a gray planet. Our environment apparently is flat going downhill. . . . What's the message? We are fouling our own nest.[27]

All this suggests what international and national priorities ought to be about during these decades: reversing the trend of fouling our nest.

> Recent research indicates that the destruction of the world's forests may actually be turning land biota into a net source of CO_2. What that means is that by destroying woodlands, we are forcing CO_2 to remain in the atmosphere rather than permitting it to be consumed by plants as a part of the photosynthesis process. It has been estimated that the clearing of forests and the decay of humus may effectively add as much CO_2 to the atmosphere annually as the burning of fossil fuel.[28]

This buildup results from a slight imbalance in the way carbon moves around between four natural reservoirs. The atmosphere itself contains about 700 giatonnes (GT) of carbon in the form of carbon dioxide (a GT equals 1000 million tons); the living matter of the earth, mainly forests, holds about 800 GT; dissolved carbon dioxide in the oceans contains 40,000 GT; and the fossil-fuel deposits on earth contain about 12,000 GT of carbon, the remains of once-living matter.[29]

We could burn all of this fossil fuel over a long period without seriously changing the carbon-dioxide concentration of the atmosphere or the climate. Eventually, the oceans will dissolve all the excess carbon dioxide produced by human activities. The problem is that it takes the seas a thousand years or more to dissolve the surplus that is being produced by humankind in the space of a few decades. At present, the oceans are absorbing about half of the extra carbon dioxide produced by human activities each year, which leaves plenty to cause climatic problems.

From 1850 to 1950, about 60 GT of carbon in the form of carbon dioxide was put into the atmosphere by burning fossil fuel, mainly coal. But over the same period about twice as much carbon dioxide was released by forest clearance and slash-and-burn agriculture. Today forest clearance in the tropics may still be adding a small amount of carbon dioxide to the atmosphere each year, but fossil fuel is the dominant influence. We are currently burning five GT of carbon each year, and the rate of fossil-fuel use is itself increasing at about 4 percent per annum. If the growth in fossil fuel use continues, the buildup of carbon dioxide in the atmosphere will double its pre-Industrial Revolution level within 50 years from now. That will be sufficient to change dramatically the patterns of global agriculture and politics.[30]

No one knows for sure what climate changes a doubling of carbon dioxide concentrations would bring. But the best of the current computer models of the atmosphere agree that, in round terms, doubling the carbon dioxide concentration will bring a rise in average temperature between two and three degrees centigrade. Even that might not look too bad, but it seems that there would be only a small increase in temperatures in the tropics and a rise of six to eight degrees centigrade or more at high latitudes.

There would also be changes in the pattern of rainfall around the world. Again, there is some uncertainty about how the rainfall patterns of a warmer world would change. But by looking at the differences between warm and cold years in the recent past, a research group at the University of East Anglia (Great Britain) has found persuasive hints that both the grain-growing regions of North America and the plains of the U.S.S.R. would have less rain, as well as higher temperatures than today, thus initiating drought. Dust bowls would become more common. The U.S.S.R. is already a major importer of grain today, and most of the world's surplus grain comes from North America. So, the pattern of climatic changes outlined by the University of East Anglia, and supported by other groups around the world, is one of the worst imaginable in terms of present global politics.[31]

There are many serious problems involved in this early debate. We know very little about these planetary matters, and our tools are still primitive. For one thing, half of the known CO_2 cannot be accounted for. Only 50% of CO_2 from fossil-fuel combustion can be accounted for. Where is the rest? The forests and grassy plains have not absorbed it. Perhaps ocean plant life is absorbing more than the oceanographers can measure at this time. No one is sure. But the underlying questions are: How much can be absorbed and for how long and with what eventual result?

There is a consensus on this point. A doubling of atmospheric CO_2 will lead to a warming of our climate on the order of more than three degrees Fahrenheit in general, and in the polar regions, much more.[32] After this, negative feedback takes place. More melting leads to more solar absorption and more melting.

Reid Bryson from the University of Wisconsin's Institute of Environmental Studies believes that the greenhouse effect will be overshadowed by negative changes in the transparency of the atmosphere, producing a cooling trend. These changes are a consequence of spreading deserts—land clearing with subsequent blowing of soil particles into the air, making the atmosphere less transparent and thereby reducing solar penetration to the earth's surface. He points to the correlation of cool weather in the early 1900s and extensive volcanic activity. Stephen Schneider of the National Center for Atmospheric Research at Boulder believes Bryson underestimates the impact of human-produced dust from agriculture, autos, aircraft, and factories. Particles cause refraction of light away from the earth.

Other climatologists and earth physicists believe one cancels out the other and that weather will remain rather consistent with the recent past. Yet a consensus exists that growing populations with growing needs and stress relationships to the ecosystem can aggravate both CO_2 and atmospheric particulate concentrations. It is difficult to determine whether the ultimate impact will be a cooling or a warming trend. Records are not clear, and theory is difficult to develop and test. The records of climate in patterns of tree rings or polar ice cores are of a period prior to a billion persons and the tools of their technologies. There is a consensus, however, that predictions are hard to make except for the negative impact of such catastrophies as nuclear war, a large meteorite striking the planet (with vast emissions of dust), or widespread and massive volcanic eruption.

But perhaps patterns of impact on weather will be neutralized by the natural historical cycles of the earth's orbit around the sun and the tilt of its axis. Perhaps not. Dr. Stephen Schneider describes it this way:

> There are always people who say that we do not know exactly what will happen . . . and they will always be right. But, the question is: what proofs must be submitted and at what risk can we proceed? [33]

He suggests:

> Since the consequences of a climatic change at the higher end of the current estimate could be both enormous and possibly irreversible, perhaps society would be best to err conservatively in planning future fossil fuel consumption patterns.[34]

The reality of CO_2 buildup (like the other constraints) is one which we cannot ignore. If you kick the system at one point, it will bulge at the other. As for myself, every time I light a fire to make a cup of tea, hear the compressor motor kick on in my refrigerator (drawing electrical current from a not-too-distant oil-fired generation plant), or use my automobile, I am conscious of the wide context of the CO_2 question. This is why I plant trees, walk as much as I can, and why my wife and I make sure that when we have a cup of tea or a bowl of soup, we have it at the same time. This is why I have encouraged my children, as well as young agricultural students and the new wave of church leaders I am privileged to serve, to have in their training opportunities and experiences that enable them to live with these concerns and sensitivities and to search for preferred values, life-styles, and strategically significant career choices.

4 Political and Economic Realities

Beyond the stress and loss of soil, agricultural lands, air, and water that has put U.S. agriculture into a state of serious crisis, complex political and economic realities must be taken into account. These realities must be understood and brought into perspective with other issues.

Fossil-fuel energy dependence in U.S. agriculture

Since World War II, we have created an incredibly high standard of living in the United States. Agriculture is a part of this record. Nowhere in the world can one find fewer farmers feeding more people. According to one study, the ratio is one farmer to 50 people—not counting the fact that about 25% to 30% of our agricultural production is going into the export market to feed millions more.[1] According to *Time* magazine the ratio is more likely to be 1 to 75.[2]

Between 1950 and 1960 U.S. agricultural production increased dramatically, even though the actual amount of land used for crop production declined. Many factors were involved. Most important, however, agriculture was based on modest energy costs. This was followed by genetic engineering for high-yielding varieties responding favorably to high inputs of chemical fertilizers. This was, of course, accompanied by mechanical advances in agricultural engineering. Regardless of the impressive ratios of farmers feeding more people, we have to ask: What are the ultimate costs to ourselves and to the world at large for this spectacular achievement?

If every nation followed the American practice in food production, processing, and distribution, all known gas and oil reserves would be used up in about 11 years.[3] In other words, all presently available gas and oil would have to be used strictly for agricultural production, food processing, and distribution purposes to feed the world's present population of more than four billion people.[4]

This figure does not take into account that to keep abreast with losses in soil erosion and fertility, more fertilizer is being applied annually to maintain present high levels of production that peaked in the early 1970s. Between 1949 and 1968 the United States increased its use of fertilizer by 648%. By the end of World War I, the average corn yield was 50 bushels per acre. Twenty-four years later, 95 bushels were harvested. We used then about 10,000 tons of chemical fertilizer, but 20 years later more than 400,000 tons were used.[5] Today, chemical fertilizers (products involving massive amounts of natural gas in the manufacture of nitrogen) account for about one-fifth of the total amount of natural gas used in the United States for all purposes.[6]

But the most cruel impact of it all is that, given the spiraling costs of oil and gas and the growing demand for these exhaustible resources, most of the more than 100 food-deficit nations have already been forced out of the petroleum market. These are the very same nations that have adopted the energy-dependent high-yielding varieties developed and introduced during the Green Revolution. The United States uses three times as much fossil-fuel energy (liquid and gas) per capita for food production than is expended in all the developing countries for all their energy-consuming activities (agriculture, industry, transportation, urban power).[7] For all of its energy requirements, the United States consumes 29% of the world's produced fossil fuel each year.[8] Yet there are more than 160 nations competing for this resource. If oil alone were used to power all U.S. activities, U.S. oil reserves would be gone in five years.[9]

Here in the United States, our energy requirements for agriculture represent only 16.5% of our total energy budget.[10] This breaks down to an equivalent of about 1400 liters of oil per capita per year for food in our food system. This percentage may not seem too high (about 6% of our total energy budget is used in the farm production process itself), but, 1) pressures on oil and gas supplies are intense within every sector of our society, 2) energy needs in agriculture are intensifying, 3) our dependence on foreign oil continues, 4) prices remain high for oil and consequently food, 5) total liquid oil and gas reserves will be largely exhausted by the end of this century or the early part of the next, and 6) we have little vision, particularly in agriculture, for a postpetroleum society.

Pimentel and his team of researchers at Cornell University developed lists of fossil-fuel energy inputs (in kilocalories) in the various farm activities in ratio to the net output of protein kilocalories. These figures represent all farm power-operations for land preparation, fertilizers, pest control, seeding, cultivating, irrigating, harvesting, and livestock feeding. The energy used is measured up to the farm gate at the time of harvest, when it is consigned to the processing and distribution system.

Milk	36:1
Eggs	20:1
Broilers	19:1
Pork	35:1
Range Beef	10:1
Feedlot Beef	78:1
Lamb (range)	16:1
Corn	1:2
Rice	1:1.6
Soybean	1:4
Drybean	1:1.8
Peanuts	1:1.4
Apples	2:1
Oranges	3:1
Potato	1:2.1
Spinach	5:1
Tomato	2:1
Sugar Beets	1:3.6
Alfalfa	1:6
Hay	1:5
Corn Silage	1:4
Fish (inshore)	103:1
(offshore)	39:1
(average after junk-fish)	27:1

When it comes to food processing, preservation, distribution, travel to and from the supermarket, and cooking, the ratios rise to as much as 1000:1 (sometimes more). For example, 15,675 kilocalories are used in the production of one kilogram of breakfast cereal, which amounts to about 3,600 kilocalories of food energy. 3011 kilocalories of energy are represented in the production of a 455 gram can of corn which has 375 kilocalories of food energy. Whether it is cornflakes, canned corn, corned beef, or corn-fed beef, the ratios run about the same.[11]

How did we get into this situation? In 1930, 80% of the world's commercial energy came from coal and gas. Even to 1950, coal still provided 60% of the world's commercial fuel. But from then until now, oil and gas have come to furnish 75% of the world's commercial energy needs.[12] In agriculture during this same period we experienced the transition from horses and mules and a few tractors to a highly mechanized system that now takes about 80 gallons equivalent to produce one acre of dryland corn.[13] The amount rises radically under irrigated conditions. In addition, most corn growers use more energy in the form of nitrogen fertilizer than in tractor fuel per acre (940,800 versus 797,000).[14] One ton of anhydrous ammonia represents in its production process from 36,000 to 40,000 cubic feet of natural gas.[15] The natural gas equivalent for Ohio's annual corn crop is equal to the amount needed to heat the homes and offices of Washington, D.C., for two winter seasons.

Fossil-fuel energy came to replace human and animal labor inputs in U.S. agriculture shortly before and during World War I. Fuel was relatively cheap. One gallon of gasoline represents 97 hours of human labor. A strong person can cultivate about one hectare of corn by hand—requiring about 1000 hours labor from soil preparation to harvest. So it is not difficult to see how fuel became a multiplier and what 1000 gallons of gasoline equivalent can mean in terms of agricultural production. Today it is not difficult for one person to manage 100 hectares of corn. Pimentel put it this way:

Fossil fuel has helped mankind manipulate ecosystems more effectively and efficiently for food production than ever before and has contributed to improving the standard of living in many parts of the world.[16]

The question is then raised: for how long and at what real cost to us and the future can this story continue?

Our standard of living (and production technologies to support this standard) is 30 to 50 times over what it was prior to World War I. Ample and cheap fuel supplies made this all possible, as well as keeping up with rising national and world populations and their spiraling resource demands, particularly for food, which 50 years ago was half of what it is today.

Now we realize the real costs, and the questions are before us everywhere: What about food prospects for tomorrow? What are our options when cheap, readily available fuel is gone, populations will be beyond six billion, soil fertility greatly diminished, and as yet, no viable agricultural production and food alternatives are being developed on a widespread basis? What are to be our strategies?

In *Rays of Hope,* Denis Hayes states: "Energy is rapidly becoming the most critical variable in the world's food system." [17]

In *New Roots for Agriculture* Wes Jackson used a time line of one year as the basis for giving perspective on energy use in United States agriculture. During this "telescoping year," as he calls it, oil had been in the process of formation for eight months. It was three seconds before midnight on the last day of the year that

> a new stream of oil began to flow throughout the country, and out of it fossil fuel . . . was discovered and was about to be used up in six seconds. It was used as feedstock for chemical fertilizers, insect control and energy for tractors in the fields. Clearly, a very new thing was happening on earth. Production of living plants was shifting from total dependence on soil to an increasing dependence on fossil fuel.[18]

The issue of contemporary agriculture's nearly complete dependency on one of the world's nonrenewable resources is grave. We are agonizingly slow even to begin the search for alternatives.

The Pimentel group concludes their study with the question: "What of the future?" Their analysis shows that even now energy, land, and other biological resource limitations make it impossible to provide the present world population of four billion with a U.S. per capita diet of 73 grams per day of animal protein. They estimate that the world's resources could support only one billion persons at this rate. They suggest that the standard of living in the world will have to be reduced to accommodate rapidly growing numbers of human beings everywhere. This then assumes 1) substantial shifts in diet (more grains, potatoes, beans), 2) smaller living quarters, 3) a slower pace in the improvement in the quality of life, 4) a critical need to control population numbers, and 5) an aggressive development of policies and programs that are ecologically sound, assuming a primary emphasis upon the augmentation of food supplies and improvement of health and education.[19] This is an awesome conclusion. Likewise, this is an awesome recommendation—a recommendation so obvious, but so effectively ignored in most nations, including our own.

Constraints on U.S. agriculture begin to take form—fossil-fuel energy will remain in abundance for about 50 more years, possible soil exhaustion will occur in 200 years, and (assuming atmospheric buildup of carbon dioxide will not curtail production and use, a most tentative assumption at best), coal and shale/oil stocks will last for 400 years. These are general estimates based on present trends in use of these resources and predictions on continual growth of demand on them.[20]

Rural community and agricultural infrastructure

The health and vitality of rural community, farmers, farm families, and essential agricultural infrastructures, like all other constraints that have been examined, are extremely complex and difficult to measure and evaluate. But, an attempt must be made. Here I am indebted to a most helpful book, *Farming the Lord's Land*, edited by Charles P. Lutz. It provides a solid overview of what is happening in the rural sector.[21]

Out-migration from rural to urban America came in the post-World War II period. Between the end of the war and the early 1970s (a period of 30 years), 30 million people left farms and rural communities for urban and industrial centers. This is considered to be one of the largest migrations of people in the history of any nation.[22] The numbers of farms and ranches dropped from roughly 6 million in 1945 to 2.6 million in 1979. During the period of 1979 to 1980, the average loss of farms and ranches was in the 100,000 range. The number of people living in rural America declined from over 50% of the population in 1920 to only 30% in 1970. About 4% of these people are actually farming and ranching. This population shift continued unabated through the 1950s and 1960s but finally began to reverse itself slightly by the early 1970s.[23]

Although 30% of the total population of the United States is rural, this group is still exploited and neglected. Of America's poor, 44% are rural, and 66% of U.S. substandard housing is found in the rural sector. But only 27% of federal welfare financial support and funds for poverty programs is committed to the rural sector.[24]

Over the past generation, farmers and ranchers have consistently received farm prices at or below costs of production. Rural branch rail lines have been abandoned. Local units of government at the township and county level have been shortchanged. Rural America has only 12% of the nation's doctors and 18% of its nurses. Only 17% of federal spending for employment and job training programs is received in rural areas. Of particular significance is that more than 30% of the nation's population 65 years and over resides in rural areas but receives only 25% of federal outlays for Social Security and other retirement programs.[25] Education is also shortchanged. About one-third of all students in U.S. public schools are enrolled in rural districts. Yet the former Department of Health, Education, and Welfare provided rural schools with only 5% of its research dollars, 11% of library and material funds, and 13% of basic vocational aid funding. Riedel and Wefald said in 1980:

> Incredibly, there is not any division or bureau within HEW to serve rural school children. Indeed, there is not one single federal employee in the Office of Education designated a rural school specialist to relate the needs of 33% of all American school children who are enrolled in rural districts.[26]

Today a person can major in urban studies in over 130 colleges and universities in this nation. But there is no integrated program in any state university where one can major in rural studies, even though rural America has over 70 million people. It is no wonder that federal and state agencies repeatedly hand down decisions and propose rules and regulations that result in the closing of too many rural schools, rural post offices, rural branch rail lines, rural hospitals, and rural businesses. One of the reasons for this is that for the past 50 years we have been producing a great and impressive variety of urban specialists in education, economics, government, housing, transportation, poverty assistance, and health care. However, few, if any, major universities are training men and women as rural specialists who have a comprehensive and in-depth grasp of the issues being identified in this book.[27] The same can be said about major centers of theological studies in the United States and attitudes and levels of administrative skills within the American church institutions.

As I have observed all around the world, and in my own nation too, agriculture is the most complex, costly, fragile, and unwanted stepchild in the whole complex of national structures, and it rests upon the shoulders of the most neglected and frequently misunderstood sector of the population, those who carry the heaviest burden of responsibility for the welfare of a nation and its future.

One does not have to look very far for reasons why the social, economic, and environmental context of agriculture is in disarray, or why the history of U.S. agriculture is one more chapter in the global record of *The Conquest of the Land Through 7000 Years*.[28] One does not have to look very far for background reasons for the existence of dysfunctional U.S. agricultural farm structures such as tax and price structures, marketing mechanisms, patterns of food processing and distribution, international agricultural commodity marketing, and agricultural research design.[29]

One does not have to search very far for understanding about how we have come to abuse the land so completely. Most decisions are now made in the cities of the nation by people with urban and industrial orientations. The words of the late Hubert Humphrey of Minnesota are prophetic:

> The truth is that rural America, with the exception of a few of us who want to take up the burden, is forgotten. I mean most of the people in government come out of the great universities, they get a fine education, and by the time they are through with it, what they know about rural America has been flushed out, and they come back with an entirely different set of values and thinking.[30]

The same can be said, generally speaking, about those not only in government but in business, finance, the arts, and the physical and social sciences. The void of knowledge and loss of sensitive leadership is a serious weakness in the fabric of our national health and environmental security. In his paper "Structure and Meaning in American Agriculture," Jerry Moles decried the loss of farm leadership. He recalled the model of Thomas Jefferson, who first discussed the nature of agriculture and society and discussed the benefits of a strong, free, and independent farm sector. Jefferson set the stage for the Homestead Act, the Land Grant Act, and a national Department of Agriculture. That kind of leadership, states Professor Moles, has disappeared.[31]

America has a long way to go before it overcomes its rural neglect—a legacy of urban and industrial orientation of recent years and which gained momentum during the administration of Secretary of Agriculture Earl Butz. His now famous quotation of 1965 sums it up quite well:

> Adapt or die: resist and perish . . . agriculture is now big business. Too many people are trying to stay in agriculture that would do better some place else.[32]

And so, corporate agriculture moved ahead while the family farm declined. The phenomenon of corporate farming is about 20 years old. A corporate farm can be defined as a large, company-owned farm, owned by nameless stockholders and operated by salaried management and labor, found mainly in the Southwest and California. Management is diluted. Most of the business is financed on annual borrowing. There is a tendency to expand—sometimes with an air of ruthlessness—onto neighboring farms, to control water and power, and to establish a vertical integration of the harvesting, processing, and marketing function. There is a heavy dependence on migrant workers (many undocumented). Corporate operations are mainly involved in "factory farming," in poultry, feedlots, canning crops, and seed crops.[33]

In contrast is the "family farm," an agricultural production unit in which the management, economic risk, and most of the labor (peak season being an exception) are provided by a given family and from which that family receives the bulk of its earnings. A family farm can range in size from a one-acre tobacco allotment in North Carolina to a Kansas wheat spread of several thousand acres. A family farm is not defined in terms of acreage, but of independent entrepreneurship.[34]

The corporate farming system is running into problems of labor relations, spiraling costs, strikes, drops in production, increased food prices, lower efficiency, and problems of stewardship of land and water resources. The operation includes large machinery, high energy inputs, specialization in crops or livestock, the elimination of fence rows and windbreaks, and a heavy reliance on fertilizers, pesticides, and herbicides. Tax shelters and price and crop subsidies are big incentives for the nonfarmer farm investor. For example, in 1978 nearly one-half of the total U.S. farm commodity payments of 2.03 billion dollars went to just 10% of the farms—the biggest. Fifty percent of the farmers—those with the smallest farms—received only 10% of these payments.[35]

As the nation ponders its agricultural future—its food supply, the struggle for survival of rural communities of people, and its agricultural natural resource base—the Earl Butz slogan, "Resist *and* perish," takes on a different, and opposite, meaning. If we resist the consideration of limits, responsibilities, real costs, values, relationships, and regard for the future, then indeed we perish.

Dispelling common myths

Before examining some of the possibilities for coping with our present crisis, we must dispel five common myths about American agriculture.

Myths	Realities
Agriculture has problems.	Agriculture is the problem.
We have a moral responsibility to feed the world.	The world needs to feed itself.
United States agriculture is productive and efficient.	United States agriculture awaits its renaissance.
Rural America is a bastion of democracy and free enterprise.	Rural America does not count any more.
The world needs to know how we do it.	United States technology should not be exported.

1. *Agriculture has problems.*

The first myth is dispelled by a most refreshing statement by Wes Jackson:

> Most analyses of the problems in agriculture do not deal with the problem of agriculture.[36]

Discussions in government, colleges, universities, on the farm, and in the urban household are about problems associated with the way farming is done. There is very little talk about the threat that agriculture makes to the stability of the biosphere itself. Agriculture is never talked about within its context of 7000 years of civilization's "conquest of the land." We talk about fragments of the problem, but never see them in relationship to the whole. As one steps back a few paces and takes a look at the whole, using global, historical, and biblical perspectives about relationships and responsibilities in God's creation, then the myth about problems within agriculture is seen for what it is and we begin to meet the whole problem straightforwardly. We are beginning to see that agriculture, as it is practiced today, as well as in the past, *is* the problem. A whole new approach, new technology, and new infrastructures are required.

2. *We have a moral responsibility to feed the world.*

The second myth that enables us to perpetuate the problem of hunger and malnutrition is that we have a moral responsibility to feed the world. To be morally responsible, we ought to say that we all have a responsibility, as partners in the whole community of creation, to enable every nation to feed *itself* on a sustainable basis. We applaud the notion that it is better to teach a person to fish than to give a fish. This is the right direction. But we had better evaluate what is taught before teaching. At this point, the metaphor about teaching people to fish runs its course of usefulness. As long as we hide behind this myth, we perpetuate paternalism and dependence, and we exceed the sustainable carrying capacity of our ecosystem.

3. *United States agriculture is productive and efficient.*

This myth leads us on toward resource exhaustion. We must count the costs of production. We have to have new criteria for defining and measuring the word "efficient." Is there efficiency in soil and energy inputs in relation to the return on the investment? Is it efficient to call nature's capital "income," leaving very little, if anything, for the inheritance of future generations?

The reality behind this myth of productivity and efficiency is that U.S. agriculture awaits its renaissance. No substantial work in research and development beyond high responsiveness to petrochemicals has been initiated. We are still developing ideas of 35 to 40 years ago when chemical fertilizers came into vogue. Our agricultural college and university faculties are overburdened with increased class enrollments, administrative responsibilities, and research commitments to agricultural activities that have already indicated their limits. Very meager state and federal funds for more sustainable farming systems have been allocated. Nothing significant is being done in the direction of state and federal extension services to America's farming community—services which laid the foundation, in the past century, for a progressive agriculture. The momentum is diverted and needs to be turned back on course.

> Agricultural research institutions have, in interaction with economic forces, cultural preferences, and other public policies, had a major influence upon our agricultural industry, and they, in turn, have been shaped chiefly by decisions of the industry subsystem. Inside this subsystem there has been agreement on some research goals, such as reducing human labor in agriculture and, in general, increasing agricultural productivity

per unit of output (although some farm groups have blamed researchers when large supplies have caused low prices), while other potential research goals have been explicitly discouraged, among them those of preserving the physical environment, encouraging rural community development, and improving consumer nutrition.[37]

4. Rural America is a bastion of democracy and free enterprise.

The fourth myth is beginning to collapse. The reality is that rural America does not really count any more. The votes are in the city. The major decisions are made in the board rooms. The essential inputs for production, as well as the markets, are vertically integrated. It was during the Arab oil crisis that a real glimpse of this reality came through. Following their own sense of fairness, the petroleum companies allocated fertilizers to America's farmers. Our lines of dependence and determination became quite clear.

5. The world needs to know how we do it.

It should be evident today, within the context of the agricultural crisis, that the world does not need to know how we do it, technologically or socially. U. S. farm technology should not be exported. Of course, the training of scientists to do original research in pest control, breeding, and soil management is essential. But the applied American technology developed from these basic sciences should be left behind.

This notion has yet to catch on. Almost everywhere I have traveled in the more than 50 food-deficit nations, I see temperate-zone technology putting people off the land, as well as contributing to the encroachment of deserts on every continent.

In the winter academic quarter of 1980, I taught a special nine-week course on the problems and potentialities of tropical agriculture in one of the agricultural colleges of the California State University system. Toward the end of the quarter I presented a film on cotton production in Costa Rica. It described the impact of aerial spraying of various pesticides on an almost daily basis on a several-thousand acre plantation. Fish were killed in adjacent rivers, streams, and even in the estuaries along the Pacific coast. People (farm workers, children, village dwellers) were hospitalized constantly. Worst of all, a resistant strain of malaria-bearing mosquito had developed along the bordering regions of the cotton-growing areas (where most of the people lived), and the incidence of malaria had quadrupled in a large section of the population. The local fish supply had been killed. Nutritional levels had dropped. Sickness and disease had spread, wages were low, and food became scarce and costly. Cotton, grown for the export market on the part of local and international investors, was being grown in a climatic setting of high rainfall and humidity. Insect control required spraying after almost every (frequent) heavy rain. Soil fertility was difficult to maintain because of the leaching and run-off effects of high rainfall on tropical soils. But, the immediate yields per acre were impressive. It was a viable economic unit. Investment capital paid good returns to the owners.

During the discussion session following the film, one student remarked: "Isn't the social and environmental cost pretty high?"

A second student replied: "Sure, but these are the trade-offs that one must be willing to accept in order to realize a profit."

I am not convinced that this attitude is unique. To the contrary, I find it a prevailing and dominant rationale in agriculture today.

We must break through the haze of our myths, because they inhibit us from developing a breadth of vision and understanding about the problem of agriculture and where solutions might be found.

Farm policy

John G. Peters, professor of political science at the University of Nebraska, contends that farm policy reflects the interests, wisdom, insights, and vision of Congress, the president, and the farm constituency (the farmer, rural community, and urban consumer). As a result, we observe through the years a "constrained discussion" about supports, markets, small and large farm interests, and social philosophy.

The discussion is further governed by national and world

demands. Nowhere does the discussion address the larger issues which I refer to as "constraints on American agriculture." Discussion about U. S. agriculture takes place in the House and Senate agricultural committees, subcommittees, the lobbying core, and interest groups. This discussion ultimately takes the form of agricultural food and farm policy.

There is a double emphasis. The first is on small farms, the rural community, social welfare, and the democratic society. The second is on the market needs of large producers and crop-production efficiency. Efforts are constant in the area of stabilized farm income, commodity production, and surplus, with a peripheral struggle about who farms, what is farmed, and how much is farmed.

Each presidential administration makes its emphasis. In the Truman years, it was on flexible but permanent controls on parity, with an eye on the welfare of the small family farm. The defeat of the Brannan plan by powerful interest groups shifted the emphasis away from the small producer. During the years of overproduction in the Eisenhower era, the emphasis was on the soil bank and acreage reserves. This was later undone by the international food crisis of the late 1960s and early 1970s. During the Kennedy and Johnson years, the emphasis was on supply management, a flexible version of parity policies. The Nixon years instituted an emphasis on a market-oriented farm program. Legislation to protect the small farmer was weakened to the advantage of the large producers. The Ford administration felt the decline of worldwide prices for agricultural commodities and the beginning of the farmer strike movement. Policy was made around commodity interests in cotton, wheat, soybean, corn, meat, and dairy products.

During the 1970s the global situation was one of food deficits. The shift was made from small farmers to agribusiness activities. During this time, budgets and grants were cut for agricultural research for the benefit of the public sector, while the private corporate sector did its own research and development. During these years the Poor People's Campaign for school lunches emerged under the leadership of Ralph Abernathy. The Senate Select Committee on Nutrition and Human

Need was developed under the leadership of Senator George McGovern.

Now in the 1980s there is a growing concern in the fields of consumer protection, land and water use, and tax structures.

All of these issues are of critical importance. But they all illustrate the thesis of this chapter: that we are yet to identify agriculture *as a problem*. We only see problems *within* agriculture. Consequently, we fail to see the larger issues, which are referred to as constraints, coming down on us now and on the future. The more significant dimensions of policy for needed reform will be identified in Chapter 8.

PART 2

The Needed Ethic
for a New Agriculture

In the earliest writings we find that the prophet and
scholar alike have lamented the loss of soils and have
warned people of the consequences of their wasteful
ways. It seems that we have forever talked about land
stewardship and the need for a land ethic, and all the
while soil destruction continues, in many places at an
accelerated pace. Is it possible that we simply lack
enough stretch in our ethical potential to evolve a set
of values capable of promoting a sustainable
agriculture?

WES JACKSON

A thing is right when it tends to preserve the
integrity, stability, and beauty of the biotic
community. It is wrong when it tends the other way.

ALDO LEOPOLD

5 Ancient Wisdom for New Problems

We are asking an awesome question in this book: Will there be food for tomorrow? The outcome of the world food crisis, as well as the future course of American agriculture, depends on whether the constant resource abuse of the world can be stopped. This hoped-for reversal depends most fundamentally on whether we humans are able to shift from relating to the sustaining resources of the created world as objects of exploitation to seeing resources as subjects of God's order.

But is reversal possible? Where can we get help? The ancient wisdom of the biblical tradition provides a firm basis for building a needed ethic for our time. In this wisdom are found fundamental insights for establishing the criteria (value, attitude, measurement, policy) for a new agriculture, an agriculture that can move us beyond the dominant destructive trends of contemporary practice into a preferred future.

The challenges to survival in the 20th century (nuclear arms proliferation; industrial pollution of the land, sea, and air; runaway population growth; desertification; soil, forest, and mineral loss; and atmospheric change) were not the challenges of the biblical period between 2000 and 3000 years ago. There are, of course, no specific biblical references to these issues. But, far more important, biblical texts contain basic and timeless insights about the relationship of humanity to the whole created world and the cosmos itself.

The biblical world view includes an understanding of the interconnectedness and dependencies of all of creation — between living things and the elemental preconditions essential for life and continued relationship. In our time and culture this view is revolutionary, because we have turned this biblical world view on its head. Our technology shows us how we can get from the world what we want. We look elsewhere for values on how we relate to the world and how its elemental resources essential for our sustenance relate to us.

Old Testament perspectives on creation

The concerns of the biblical period of history are both similar and dissimilar to ours. The similarity is that people then and now asked the same questions about ultimate purpose, meaning, and relationship that have challenged the imagination of the human species for several millenia.

Significantly, the word *nature* does not exist in either Old or New Testament texts. There is no equivalent in the Scriptures. The New Testament uses the word *creation* in place of *nature* to include all of life. The ancient Hebrews did not separate humanity from the rest of creation. Both Old and New Testaments assume the unity of creation and emphasize the decisive role humans play in the process of creation. According to the Bible, creation is all one piece. The basis for this unity is the relationship of all creation with God.[1]

The mandate to have dominion over the rest of creation is misunderstood if we do not appreciate that we too are a part of that creation.[2] The trees are brought forth from the earth and given to us for food. We are born of the soil and receive our sustenance from it.[3] We belong to this world completely. It bears us, nourishes us, and holds us.[4]

God creates nature not only for our sakes but also that God might take joy in it and serve all its creatures.[5] According to Israel's creation theology, it would be going too far to say that the world is created only for the sake of humankind. God saw everything that God made and said: "very good" (Gen. 1:31). Every creature, including humanity, is assigned its proper place and function in God's creative order so that all creation serves and glorifies the Creator.[6] Nonhuman life praises and honors God (Ps. 19:1ff; Isa. 40:26). God delights in nature and cares for it, quite apart from its importance for human beings (Job 38-39; Ps. 104:10ff). For the Hebrews any purely utilitarian attitude toward the nonhuman world would be irreligious; a wanton exploitation of the nonhuman created order or indifference to its beauty and delicate balances would constitute an affront to God.[7]

God is the creator of the universe. God is the sole source of everything that exists. Indeed, there is no material substance which can exist independently of the creative will of God. Creation is the world. According to the Bible, the world belongs to God, not to humanity. Creation—including elemental creation (rocks, water, air)—is for the support of the human species, as well as for all other life forms. God created life for all life and for its perpetuation. Life is God's gift, understood in the Bible as the miracle of creation. This whole creation is God's; life is a gift; and nothing exists for the exclusive disposal of one form of life or another. All creation points to the one who is worthy of praise.[8] Creation consists not only of human beings and the earth but includes the planets, stars, and galaxies.[9] Reading from Isaiah one sees that Yahweh created the earth and its produce (42:5). He formed the heavens and maintains the planets in their courses (40:22, 26). But in addition to fashioning the physical world, he gives breath to the people upon it and spirit to those who walk in it (42:5). Yahweh can change the appearance of the creation. He can make the wilderness a pool of water, and make the pine and cedar flourish in the desert wastes (41:18-19).

In the semiarid world of the Old Testament life was totally dependent on rainfall which came during the six winter months. The soils were very permeable, holding little groundwater. There was little forest, only sparse vegetation suitable for the grazing of small animals. Permanent human settlements were rare; only seminomadic life was possible. Main crops were millet, wheat, barley, beans, lentils, some vegetables, tree crops, and vines. All in all, it was a very modest life-style. This biogeographical setting predetermined Israel's perception of the world about it. This understanding, or world view, was one of wonderment and delight over Yahweh's blessing. Meager though the blessing was, it was God's gift.

Humanity does not have responsibility for shaping existence. It is only God who determines what is good for humanity. When humankind shapes the world to meet its own particular interests, the world depreciates. Therefore, salvation rests in working with Yahweh within an understanding of the creative process.[10]

These texts present creation as a breathtaking vision of an interdependent world. All distinction between the "sacred" and the "profane" has been cleared away. The whole cosmos is one great sanctuary.[11]

In the early Old Testament texts of Genesis 2-3 (the Garden of Eden), Genesis 9:18-27 (the cursing of Canaan), Genesis 10 (the table of the nations), and Genesis 11:1-9 (the tower of Babel), the world is understood as a great event, still in the process of development. All life—human, animal, plant—is part of this meaningful process. All is part of life's sphere of existence which would not be possible without God's bestowed gift, either now or for the future. In this setting, humankind has no ability to create the elemental aspects of this creation. In this creation, there is a clear sense of order. This whole ordered world is the milieu for humankind.[12]

This world is the elemental condition of life. The Old Testament texts convey the idea that one of the purposes of the world is to provide the basis for human existence. The created order provides for humanity, not for its autonomous will, but simply for its sustenance. This whole process of life is a gift Yahweh bestows, one that has value and meaning determined by Yahweh, not humankind. Humans are deluded when they think they know what is good and evil. On the contrary, such delusion causes humankind to determine its own goals autonomously in its dealings with the natural world of God's creation, and this results in damage and destruction.

In Psalm 104 a more cosmic order emerges, enlarging the human understanding. This psalm was written in urban Jerusalem during the Davidic Empire. It is a psalm about Yahweh's creative activity in the world, stressing the elemental connection between the natural world and the living things. It is a

description of the divine gift of the world, of air, sea, mountains, and valleys. It is an orderly cosmological sphere in which
all is secure. Plants, animals, humanity—all are dependent and
benefiting from the other and endowed with provisions for
life:

> These all look to thee,
>   to give them their food in due season.
> When thou givest to them, they gather it up;
>   when thou openest thy hand, they are filled with good things.
> When thou hidest thy face, they are dismayed;
>   when thou takest away their breath, they die and return to
>   their dust.
> When thou sendest forth thy Spirit [breath],
>   they are created;
>   and thou renewest the face of the ground (vv. 27-30).

The psalmist understood life as a benevolent gift of God
conferred on all life in a continuing process which is not at
the disposal of humanity. Human life is dependent on that
which humanity never did—nor can—create.[13]

> O Lord, how manifold are thy works!
>   In wisdom hast thou made them all;
> the earth is full of thy creatures (v. 24).

Clearly, in these passages, humanity has no preeminent position. Its value is no greater than any other form of created
life. The human species is a part of an order, but it is not set
apart from it. Rather, all life unfolds for the sake of the whole
creation. The psalm points to the uniqueness of human life:
it is capable of praising God but also capable of destroying,
both capabilities being quite beyond those of other life forms.

How different this is from our modern age. In the psalm, life
begins and is oriented to God's interest. In our time humanity
is inclined to believe that the world is an object to be exploited
for the interests of humankind. For the most part, we seem
oblivious to the needs of other life forms.

Between the 6th and 5th centuries B.C., Genesis 5 (the gene-
alogy from Adam to Noah), Genesis 6–8 (the flood), Genesis
9:1-17 (the blessing of Noah and the covenant), and Genesis
10 (the table of the nations) were written. Here we see a

further view of the world of God's creation. In these writings one finds a similar, though expanded, concurrence with those themes just identified. Humanity is created in God's image, which included the idea of sovereignty—the responsibility to preserve order and to promote the existence of all life.[14] In other words, humanity's task is to guarantee life's fundamental provision. Though Yahweh created and bestowed life with provisions for life, humankind is to act as governor on earth. In this sense they govern according to God's order and interests for all life.

This position of responsibility does not at all imply autonomous and autocratic freedom to dispose of the world's resources for self-chosen purposes. Rather, the responsibility is to keep the creative process alive for the good of the whole, both now and into the future. God established the framework of life; humanity is to implement it. According to these biblical writers, sovereignty meant responsibility for living together for the mutual benefit of all. This was God's will. Humanity is God's steward whose first task is to assure permanence.

In the creation accounts, the high place of human beings is affirmed. The creation of human beings made in the image of God is the climax of the creative drama. The earth was converted to a garden for human use. The animals are created to be companions for the humans, and the humans are given the authority to give them names.[15] How eloquently the writer of Psalm 8 expresses this. He claims that humanity is crowned with honor and glory, reflecting the splendor of God. Humanity is created in the image of God. Though we are ephemeral creatures in comparison to the stars, God has elevated us to be God's representatives on earth. We are the ones who can sing aloud the praise of the whole creation.[16]

Humanity's dominion over animals in Gen. 1:26-28 illustrates clearly the point of the words *subdue* and *dominion*. God created life for the sake of all life. One life form is not at the exclusive disposal of another. God places humanity as trustee or steward. Thus, humanity acts (expresses dominion over animals) according to its understanding of God's will for the whole creation.

These texts stress that humanity is created in the image of God, with the responsibility to be fruitful, multiply, to fill the earth and to subdue it, to have dominion over the fish of the sea and over the birds of the air and over every living thing that moves upon the earth. God destined us to have a special relationship with all creation.[17] To be in the image of God means that we have a particular task to perform.[18] We are in God's image not because of what we are but because we have been given a share in the divine sovereignty over creation.[19] The decisive relationship which defines and expresses the image of God in us is our relationship with the other creatures God has fashioned. To be in God's image is to be in responsible relationship with the land and all its life.[20]

In these writings God no longer is seen to be continually active in the world as creator. Consequently, humankind is to play out the role of monarch or governor. The key point is this. Humanity, in fulfilling this role, must continually test its actions against the gifts that God gave it so that the world of creation and the world of humankind can continue to live.[21] Again and again, the theme recurs: creation (the world) is not at the disposal of humanity. The world is for all life, given by God the creator in the beginning.

In summary:

1. Creation of the whole world is God's, and everything that is within it. All has quality, value, and meaning to God. All life has purpose.

2. Creation is a continuous process. It provides for all the necessities of life.

3. Creation and its miracle of life is a gift bestowed by the Creator upon all life.

4. This created world and its environment is not at the disposal of humankind. Rather, humankind is a representative of God, as a monarch within his or her domain, to act as a steward in governing the use of the resources of life, for all life, for the purpose of keeping the creative process alive and moving forward. Humankind has responsibility for liberation, for working for the establishment of a full justice that reflects cosmic order.

New Testament wisdom about creation and redemption

The New Testament is focused on its testimony to the new activity of God in the coming of Jesus Christ. This coming of Christ opens up a sphere of meaningful and fulfilled life which is not confined to the existing natural world but aims to go beyond it in God's future world. Thus, all statements made about the natural world are auxiliary to this theme.[22] But this emphasis does not come out of a vacuum. It takes place in God's incarnation and in the work of the church in the midst of the present world. The center of the New Testament proclamation is the Christ event; it is from this central focus that we look for understanding of what this means for us as witnesses in the age of crisis and survival.

Like in the Old Testament, the decisive testimony of the New Testament is in its world view. This world view provides the capacity for exercising critical power in the present and breaks through the current way of looking at things, giving a new orientation, a new way of looking at suffering and hope. The New Testament does not address the world and environment extensively. Rather, its witness has a much more specific focus. But its worldview orientations are implicitly expressed.[23]

The time and setting are quite different from the Old Testament texts previously discussed. The New Testament reflects the dispersion history. Trade, crafts, and commerce had appeared, and Christian communities were found largely in the cities of the eastern and northern Mediterranean.

The parables of Jesus, however, are built on the vivid panorama of farmers, shepherds, fishermen, and tenant farmers. Jesus made constant reference to the sun and rain (Matt. 5:45), birds of the air and lilies of the fields (Matt. 6:26, 28), humanity's dependency on food (Matt. 6:31), sheep and wolves, snakes and doves (Matt. 10:16), tilling the soil (Matt. 13ff), fishing (Luke 5:1ff), and the shepherd's life (Matt. 13:1ff.).

There is no doubt, however, that the natural world, which is there to provide for human and beast, and the gift of life itself are seen, entirely as a matter of course, as God's creative activity.

As in Old Testament history, New Testament people were quite conscious (in contrast to most people of our time) of their dependencies on the elements of the natural world and environment that were essential for life. New Testament people saw life as a gift which humans cannot extend by a single day. Jesus pointed to God the Creator in the midst of creation. Jesus saw the world as an experience of God's loving nearness, from which the proper way of living emerges, a way that is consistent with the future kingdom of God. If humankind makes this its orientation, people will walk in God's world thoughtfully. Life and creation itself take on a whole new quality in relation to the kingdom of God. For example, in the gospel of John (John 17:24), God the Creator, active in the world, is presupposed, though this theme is not explicitly developed. In Acts, the natural world is seen as the framework of creation.

> And when they heard it, they lifted their voices together to God and said, "Sovereign Lord, who didst make the heaven and the earth and the sea and everything in them . . . " (Acts 4:24).

This point of view is also expressed in Paul's speech at Athens, from Acts 14.

> Men, why are you doing this? We also are men, of like nature with you, and bring you good news, that you should turn from these vain things to a living God who made the heaven and the earth and the sea and all that is in them (Acts 14:15).

Likewise in the Pauline epistles, Old Testament orientations about the world, life, and God's creation are seen. For example, one can observe reflections of Genesis in Romans:

> As it is written, "I have made you the father of many nations"—in the presence of the God in whom he believed, who gives life to the dead and calls into existence the things that do not exist (Rom. 4:17).

The Old Testament orientation in Psalm 104 can be seen in 1 Cor. 10:26-27. Paul says that the people who make themselves subject to wrath are inexcusable because, in spite of knowing better, they pervert themselves and their world. The world is God's—a gift. The world is a sphere for human existence. In Christ, we are free with a new orientation to relate meaningfully. We see this in Romans:

> Do not be conformed to this world, but be transformed by the renewal of your mind, that you may prove what is the will of God, what is good and acceptable and perfect (Rom. 12:2).

This passage speaks of our being liberated in Christ to existence as it really is—a gift of life, for life, and not at the disposal of any one part of life. This is one of the essential meanings of liberation. Our choice is to accept God's order and full justice, which is not ours. For Paul, the Christ event expresses the universal dimension of creation.

All things made new

In the New Testament Jesus of Nazareth is the event in which God enters directly into the whole reality of the created world, of politics, economics, and the personal dimensions of human existence. Christ is portrayed as a revelation in the totality of existence. In him there is a transformed perspective directed toward all sectors of life and the elemental guarantees of the natural world. The natural world becomes the milieu of God's revelation in Jesus Christ.

In the New Testament we see a world created by God but distorted by humanity to a state of injustice and imperfection, a world which is difficult to reconcile with God's ruling power. But the new coming of God in Jesus Christ transforms this into a new history of salvation, in which hope and the conditions of hope are understood. The future is nourished by the visionary concept of the kingdom which is open to those who are liberated in Christ and transformed, not by this world, but by the vision of a future kingdom on earth.[24]

Christian faith expands our outlook for our present relationships to the world, its environment, and about prospects for the future. The New Testament calls us to see the world and its future in the light of redemption in Christ, to see the world as God's. The New Testament sees the world in three ways: the sphere of God's activity in creation, the sphere where human self-centeredness rules, and the sphere where faith emerges and transforms—where all things are made new.

The New Testament emphasizes that humanity's unbridled striving to build and preserve a self-imposed and more demanding world, while disregarding the enduring will of God for the whole life of the whole creation, is the cause of devastation. The cross unmasks the immensity of the sin of self-centeredness. In this situation the central theme of the New Testament is that humanity cannot free itself without redemption in Christ. On this point the New Testament is unanimous and uncompromising. In other words, we cannot step beyond our own selves without God's redemptive transformation in Christ. Given the existence of humanity, with its self-serving understanding of freedom and its propensity to sin, creation remains diminished, damaged, suppressed, and threatened.[25]

In Christ, in turning to God's will, the believer is no longer molded and determined by this self-centeredness. Rather, the believer is liberated from it and placed into a wider understanding of liberation, as expressed in Paul's letter to the Romans. In Christ's suffering, death, and resurrection, the believer experiences God's redemptive love. This experience activates our thinking, love, imagination, and willingness for renunciation and sacrifice in our own time and in our crises. It empowers the believer to do whatever is necessary to work soberly and steadily to preserve God's world of creation from the self-centeredness of humanity.

Jesus and the whole New Testament witness never gave way to the illusion that everyone will accept Christ in faith. Consequently, in the struggle to witness and reconcile, the believer never falls victim to the illusion that this human world can be transformed once and for all, unscathed, by the proclamation of the gospel. It is a constant task. History has set the precedent.

In the third sphere of New Testament understanding, a sphere where faith emerges and transforms and where all is made new, the believer in Christ is free in faith to witness to the connection between the divine future, the present, and the past. In Christ we are free to draw attention to the wisdom that keeps alive the sense of responsibility and accountability to God and the created world of life and process. In this sphere the believer works to create and establish models for ministry and service which reflect the signs of creation in the life and work of individuals and their associations. Believers work for it in their dealings with the natural world by confirming and supporting the elemental "givens" in creation— basic values, perceptions, directions for perception and cognition. This unfolds by showing critically what the world really is, the purpose of human life, and the course of the endangered world, in the light of the Christ event and by holding out to men and women the salvation which God in grace wants to give all created things in order to complete and perfect creation.[26]

Foundations for a new ethic

Biblical wisdom furnishes us with a foundation for building an ethic for a new agriculture. The overarching Old and New Testament theme expresses an understanding of the basic interconnections in all of creation. The maintenance of these lines of interdependency and interconnectedness is the elemental precondition for the continued existence of the miraculous gift of life.

In addition, biblical wisdom points to five basic themes:

1. Creation is God's, and it is filled with value and meaning to God.

2. Creation is a continuous process which provides for the necessities of life.

3. Life is a miraculous gift.

4. This gift is not at our disposal to do with it as we please.

5. In Christ we are empowered to make all things new.

The task before us is to relate this wisdom to contemporary concepts of agriculture as a way to critically evaluate our situation and to point a way beyond our present situation into what can be called a preferred future. Do our present technologies and attitudes about agriculture and its resource base reflect our sensitivity to the biblical understanding that all resources have meaning to God? Does our agriculture guarantee the interconnectedness of life forms and their patterns of existence, or does it go the other way? Do we relate to the miracle of life in covenant, or do we exploit it as we please? With a renewed spirit in Christ, are we committed to the renewal of agriculture so that it reflects the great themes of biblical wisdom?

6 A New Ethic
for Agriculture

Formulating an adequate definition of the word *agriculture* is not simple. As I searched the literature for assistance, I was surprised to find that little has been done to develop a comprehensive definition. What does exist is brief and covers a wide spectrum of ideas. Most definitions refer to problems in agriculture or the problem of agriculture itself, problems in farming—corporate or family—and agribusiness, with purposes focused on everything from food production to commodity trading, employment, and defense. At one extreme, for example, Earl Butz said: "Farming isn't a way of life, it's a way to make a living." [1] The *Oxford Dictionary* puts it at the other extreme: "Agriculture is the science and art of cultivating the soil." The *Random House Dictionary* states it this way: "Agriculture is the science or art of cultivating land in the raising of crops."

What is agriculture?

Is agriculture a science? Is it an art? Is it a science and an art? Is it a way of making money? Is it an activity in tillage, cultivating, and husbandry? It is all of these things and much more. One can read into these statements several meanings. However, the problem remains that meaning is restricted to the perspectives about purpose that a person brings to the definition. Bib-

lically, the Hebrew meaning of *cultivate* is "service." To cultivate the land is to serve the land—to nurture it, to take care of
it, and to participate in its productive processes. Today, however, *cultivate* refers to the various mechanical activities in
crop production, such as soil preparation, planting, weed control, irrigation (in arid settings), and pest control.

For the purpose of stretching our ethical potential to evolve
a set of values capable of promoting a sustainable agriculture,
and to set into motion a discussion of the full meaning and
implication of this definition, I have designed the following
definition. *Agriculture refers to a dynamic human process of
combining the energies of the sun with the chemistry of the
soil, vegetation, and animals, in the production of food and
fiber for the purpose of making possible the indefinite development of the potentiality of human life in community.*

Agriculture is a process.   The point of first importance in
this definition is that agriculture refers to a human process.
Agriculture is the result of human activity which combines
natural forces and life forms in the production of food and
fiber. From the time of early settled civilizations until now,
agriculture represents human initiatives. In this, it is far
different from hunting and gathering. Whether or not agriculture is sustainable or exhaustive depends on how the human
process of combining the basic components of agriculture is
accomplished. The process of agriculture, like the process of
so much of our life, has no real meaning in itself. It takes on
meaning only as value and purpose is clarified and made part
of the process.

Agriculture has a purpose.   In the normative biblical sense,
the ideas of *creation* and *covenant* suggest that the purpose
of human life is to participate in the creative process of God's
will for the life of planet earth. If we apply this basic idea
to the question of purpose in agriculture, we discover the ideal
of making possible the indefinite development of the potentiality of human life in community. This potential unfolds in
community rather than in isolation or apartness. *Community*
is a word that refers not only to human community but to the
whole community of created life and the essentials for the sus-

tenance of all of this life. Like the individual person, human community cannot develop to its potential in isolation.

The definition of agriculture revolves around the key ideas of *process* and *purpose*. But the underlying essence of both notions is the maintenance of quality relationships. Agriculture is defined, in part, as the human process of combining its many components in ways that guarantee community and its future. *Community* refers to the harmonious, interdependent, and mutually supporting *relationships* of community, of the common unity of things. Agriculture is the product of many relationships (a product in the mathematical sense), not of one aspect or another. It is the whole phenomenon of the dynamic process of combining the many components of agriculture. A product is different from the sum total. For example, seven times seven is more than seven plus seven—much more!

The essence of quality relationship is found in diversity. Security in our food systems will be built on diversity. We have to look only to the natural world about us to recognize this fact. Our security and life quality do not lie in centralized, vertical integration of ownership, authority, and decision making. They do not rest in large-scale monocultural agriculture or in the hands of less than 4% of the population of a nation. On the contrary, sustainability (a profound expression of security) in agriculture is dependent on a vast heterogeneity of social structure and biological diversity. In this, quality is to be found.

Ethical guidelines

Three ethical guidelines shape a normative definition of agriculture and a vision of a preferred agriculture: *justice, participation,* and *sustainability.* These guidelines for a preferred agriculture emerge out of the perspectives of a threatened agriculture and biosphere and an impoverished humanity. They function as foundation blocks for a responsible agriculture. They give us direction in the search for ways to reverse the destructive direction of the history of agriculture and enable us to begin to change the present course of exhaustion in agriculture. These interrelated and interdependent guidelines enable us to envision a preferred agriculture with high expectation.[2]

1. Justice

To what primary purpose and goal should our agricultural science and technology be committed? Should it be to the maintenance of favorable trade balances and the maximization of profit? Or should our purpose be the maintenance and renewal of the necessary resources for food, clothing, and shelter for both now and the future?

Is it possible to conceive of a global agricultural future without justice?

These questions are asked in human terms as well as in reference to nonhuman life. If human relationships to nonhuman forms of life are not just, can the human species (now numbering more than four billion persons and soon expanding to six billion) survive in a world community of intricate interdependencies? If forests, prairies, air, and freshwater resources—and all the intricate mechanisms that are essential for the perpetuation of these resources—become exhausted or overstressed, can we survive? As our knowledge of our dependent relationship grows, we have to place intrinsic value on an ever-increasing variety of things.

This enlarged concept of justice is the opposite of a narrow individualism in which each person is solely responsible for his or her own welfare. The task of the society is to maximize the welfare of all its members and the free development of each of them. This is possible only in a society where the people determine the purpose of the production of goods, the ways to maintain order, and the direction of the development of their culture within the delicate boundaries of the carrying capacity of the earth and of the ecosystems in which each culture is located.

Our concept of individualized freedom must recognize its obligation to future generations. We have to think through their rights against our own. From the perspective of the biblical idea of "dominion," we must see ourselves as members of the "biotic team," where equity and justice must be maintained by considering the value of all life forms.[3] By so doing, we place moral responsibility on a high plain. This makes the concept of justice very inclusive.

A just society and a just agriculture provide the means by which people can share the inheritance of the earth so that all can fully be maintained in freedom and community. For example, can a farmer produce milk and cheese from his or her dairy herd for a long time if, in the process, the pastures and fodder croplands are overburdened and destroyed in the process of maximizing production? Can a society survive in justice and dignity if it uses up its capital resources while it cheerfully refers to these resources as income? [4] Can we survive if our prevailing agricultural science and technology remains committed first of all to the idea of food for profit over a short period of time instead of the enhancement of this biosphere for our inheritance into the indefinite future?

A just agriculture (local and global) is impossible to achieve without justice at the level of community participation. In the centrally organized world that we live in today, science and technology are usually forced to be on the side of those who wield economic and political power. There are few indications that science and technology are on the side of the oppressed, the deprived, and the marginalized, or simply on the side of the people. Is agriculture, first of all, for the financial advantage of the wealthy or for meeting one of the fundamental rights of all people?

For an agriculture to be just, everyone has the right to be consulted. But herein lies the political conflict. When the social system reduces its "productive efficiency" for the sake of justice, to what extent should justice be sacrificed for efficiency? Should fragmented small holdings be consolidated to increase production? Was this not one of the fundamental arguments about the U. S. Land Reclamation Act of 1902? The argument for the enforcement of the Act suggested that people needed to be on the land, even though some observed that this was not the most efficient way to produce the food the nation and world needed. Congress chose the latter in 1980 and sacrificed the former! Farm sizes were enlarged, shutting out those who sought opportunity to own small farms. This was done in the name of "production efficiency." To what extent should to-day's governmental leaders pursue policies that enhance the possibility for justice in the future — for guaranteeing the existence of prime farmland, of soil, forest, energy, mineral supplies, and water? Is not this kind of thinking politically risky in today's world of values centered on immediate sovereignty and security for the few? What is the long-range price we must all pay in terms of social, political, and environmental stability, the sustainability of resources, and the biosphere's capacity to absorb pollution?

It is obvious that justice has to be understood at several levels. No one level is to be sacrificed for the other. It is ludicrous to think of justice for the future when it is denied in the present. But as true as this is, we must also consider justice for the future. Can we call nature's capital "income," knowing that there will be little "inheritance" for tomorrow's generations?

As we look at the interdependencies of the whole creation, and with reverence and humbleness seek to relate to the created order in wholeness as trustees of the land, we must also look at the question of justice among nonhuman forms of creation. For example, is it just to destroy an aquifer? Is it just to destroy prairies and marshlands? Is it just to destroy the whale, the porpoise, the elephant, the gazelle, the buffalo, or the pheasant and quail in the fence rows? Should we not consider God's will in keeping the creative process and purpose alive and healthy? If these kinds of different questions are not raised, then we have few guidelines to assist us in maintaining the life and health of the ongoing process of creation. We have no way to guarantee stability now or for the future.

In his understanding of the ethics of reverence for life, Albert Schweitzer saw no sharp distinction between precious and less precious life. He believed that to make these distinctions is ultimately beyond our capacity. He thought that we must refrain, as far as possible, from destroying all forms of life. Schweitzer saw that nature compels us to recognize our mutual dependence. He tried to show that each life necessarily helps the other. He saw that our human life is

related in solidarity with all forms of life. This insight is
much more than ecological enlightenment. Schweitzer understood these things from a spiritual basis. He recognized that
all living things spring from the same source, that all forms
of life have certain similarities, and that there is a "spiritual
reunion" and harmony within the creative will which is in
and throughout all life forms.[5]

In the light of Schweitzer's thought we observe the importance of interrelatedness to justice for a preferred agriculture. It becomes clear that the denial of the guideline of
justice and of the value to participate in the creative enter-
prise of God's creation and to work for a sustainable future
results in the denial of the deepest level of human rights and
the human value of responsibility. For whatever reasons
(poverty, sickness, illiteracy, or political powerlessness), to
be denied the opportunity to participate in the ongoing process
of creation is the deepest level of injustice. Is this not also the
case for the rights of nonhuman life, the denial of the right
to participate and contribute to the welfare of all life?

In the United States today young people find it almost impossible to enter farming as individual operators, because of
high costs of equipment, land, and operating capital. It is
wrong to shut out this new generation of people who want to
develop farming systems that are more participatory and
just. New generations of citizens are now being denied a most
basic human right. Our nation today must take a hard look
at the consequences of this relatively new situation in American agriculture.

2. Participation

Participation in society and in the ongoing process of creation
is the necessary condition for justice. Participation requires
a recognition of everyone's right to be consulted and understood, whatever the person's political, economic, or social
status. Participation assumes that every person has a responsibility to take initiative in formulating or changing policy
and to be involved in implementing policy. This includes decisions about such issues as armament expenditures and nuclear-
based energy production, forms of employment, opportunities

for medical services, educational structures and curriculum, and transportation systems.

What determines whether or not a society is just or sustainable is the participation in its affairs by its members. We know that material growth cannot ensure freedom and justice without the willing participation of the masses, who alone must decide what must be produced and how much.[6] Was this point not proven during the late stages of Western colonial rule, when there was material progress but without the right of participation? Was not this policy one of the causes for the collapse of colonialism? Is this not the prevailing assumption behind many of our so-called "development activities" in international aid assistance to the former colonial nations, particularly in Africa and Latin America? Can there be stability and meaning in community when decisions about the lives and destinies of communities are made in secret? Participation in decision making and planning, with justice and sustainability as the vision and central core of preferred values, overcomes the totalitarianism of "elitist" decision making.[7] We know that only when people participate in decision making does it become morally binding for all.[8]

In the Old Testament view of human life, decisions have to be made that reflect a consciousness of our interdependence with the whole of the land—its water, soil, air, animal, and vegetable forms of life. In our new history, involving upper atmospheric transportation, instantaneous communication, international production and trade, worldwide armaments and nuclear threat, participatory decisions have to be undertaken in a transnational and transcultural process.[9] The old nationalistic tradition of sovereignty in the West ought to become a thing of the past. Today every nation is connected to every other nation, like the segments of a spider's web. A push at one point affects the entire fragile structure. Look, for example, at the patterns of Chinese and French atmospheric nuclear bomb radiation across the Pacific, the United States, and Canada. The impact of rainfall patterns in the Caribbean from Sahelian dusts following the Harmaatan winds is another timely illustration.

Participation is not possible without power. Thus, a necessary condition for insuring real participation is the dispersal of power—both political and economic—avoiding its concentration in the hands of a few who are not held accountable to the norms of justice, participation, and sustainability. This is one of the urgent problems related to the phenomenon of the transnational agricultural corporations. It is the corporation that usually makes decisions with reference to community and natural environmental welfare issues in Costa Rica, the Amazon Basin, Haiti and the Dominican Republic, Bolivia, and Chile.

The lack of formal education must not be used as an excuse for preventing participation in decision making. The obvious condition for a participatory society is the uninhibited flow, not only of scientific and technical knowledge, but also of information on current affairs. The scope of participation ought to be determined by the extent of shared interests. Our interdependencies are all too obvious in our new world of science-based technology.

At the deepest level of understanding about participation we must see ourselves as coparticipants with God. This is our highest value and one closest to our idea of covenant. In new and astonishing ways we recognize that we are participants along with the myriad of all creatures in the developing process and purpose of creation.[10] For the sake of perspective we must realize that we are relative latecomers in creation, not central and sovereign (in the narrow sense of these terms), but rather coparticipants with all other forms of animate and inanimate creation, and are more accountable to God for our activities. Our decisions must be made from the perspective of the whole continuing process of creation. Outside this wider context decision making is not participatory, just, or sustainable.

3. Sustainability

An ecologically sustainable agriculture is a necessary requirement for justice and underlies the value and guideline of participation. A sustainable society and a sustainable agriculture is one where the idea of permanent carrying capacity is maintained, where yields (agricultural, forestry, energy production, industrial activity, water use) are measured on a sustainable basis rather than by the conventional criteria of the maximization of yields per acre or profit from investment. A sustainable agriculture is one in which waste products can be absorbed back into the ecosystem without damage.[11]

Sustainability is a condition for justice. In the industrialized nations the idea of sustainability provides the basis on which to judge the wasteful and polluting aspects of the consumption of nonrenewable resources. It is also the basis for evaluating heavy reliance on material growth at the expense of nonrenewable resources and material growth at the expense of the enlargement of the human spirit and justice in the social relationships.

At the global level of considering the issue of sustainability, the so-called developing nations cannot be expected to be as concerned as the industrialized world about problems of sustainability that are not of their own making. Furthermore, the concern about the welfare of unborn generations must square with the needs of the millions who are hungry today. A sense of proportion should therefore inform our perception of the relevance of sustainability to social justice. Problems that are essentially Western both in scope and responsibility must not be turned into global issues that inhibit the struggle against malnutrition and the quest for a fuller justice. For example, efforts to reduce the consumption of fossil fuel for our automobiles, aircraft, and agricultural industries must not expand to a condemnation of a desperate family in a desperate place to reduce its use of firewood to cook and make digestible its only daily meal of millet or rice. Rather, efforts to conserve and replenish resources in the rich world need to be expanded.

At the same time equal efforts need to be directed to overcoming poverty, with its consequent environmental degradation on forest and other resources in the so-called poor world. These are issues for American agriculture to ponder, particularly with reference to fossil-fuel energy use in our food production, processing, and distribution systems.

Ecosystems that are damaged or destroyed in the process of their use recover at rates from tens to hundreds of years. The coal regions of Appalachia are a good example of this. It is of prime importance for us all, inside and outside agriculture, to develop economic policies for natural resource use in the context of long-term stability rather than immediate goals. For illustrative comparison, one should study the new energy-production towns in Wyoming and Montana, or the abandoned lumber towns in the Pacific Northwest, in comparison to forest-oriented villages in Scandinavia, Scotland, France, or Germany.

To move from short-range thinking to long-term planning—using the values of justice, participation, and sustainability as guidelines—will be difficult at first because of predominant economic pressures not generally geared to these forms of thinking. In dealing with agricultural questions, preservation (renewal), a policy of sustained yield, ought to be the basis for all our actions in law and technology.

We do have the knowledge, technology, and resources to develop a sound and humane world in which basic precepts for wholesome and sustainable life systems will not be violated. We can derive some hope for the fruition of this ideal from the fact that ever-increasing numbers of people, including many leading industrialists, are becoming aware that once we discontinue our obsolete obsession with quantitative growth, we will be free to focus our efforts on a culturally more sustainable way of life.[12]

In accord with this concept of sustainability, we must value a "reserve capacity" built into every major agricultural technological system as a necessary step for survival and the prevention of sudden catastrophic collapse. We must respect the limits to which we can stress the carrying capacity of each local agricultural ecosystem and learn to live within these limits. Decentralization needs to be encouraged, even during our time when the trend is in the opposite direction.

Preferred technologies are smaller, capital-saving, less rapacious in their demands on raw materials, environmentally nonviolent, and leading toward an environmentally sustainable life-style. To maintain stability and to guarantee the future, our task is to keep alive the evolving edges of creation, the intricate regulatory mechanisms of nature, including normal radiation patterns of light entering our ozone shield; normal flows of oxygen, carbon dioxide, and nitrogen generation and absorption; a healthy soil microbiology and diversified grass-lands and forest complexes; and purity of air, sea, and water supplies. If we are to think of a sustainable future and partici-patory justice, our technology must enhance these natural cycles.

The essence of agriculture further considered

The words of microbiologist Rene Dubos are prophetic in our time. They reinforce the essence of our agricultural definition.

> We must base our actions upon value judgments on the quality of the relationship between humankind and the earth, in the future as well as in the present.[13]

This is the basic need of our time. It redirects science and technology toward the goals of quality so essential for sur-vival.[14] This idea brings together the value and the guidelines of a preferred agriculture. From the perspective of a wise and elder statesman of accomplishment in microbiology, ethics, and philosophy, Dubos is hopeful for the future because he observes that societies are now learning to anticipate the dangers of failing to deal with the issues of environmental and human exploitation and injustice. He observes that the natural re-sources of forests, grasslands, and deserts have great poten-tialities that remain unfulfilled until properly manipulated by human labor, love, and imagination. This is a courageous, forthright, and visionary position. From the perspectives of his own active, inquisitive, and hopeful life and from many great moments in history, he observes that human beings can improve on nature by manipulating it with respect, imagina-tion, and intelligence.[15]

Modern human beings have become destructive because they have lost their sense of quality and level of high responsibility for maintaining harmonious relationships to the earth. Dubos believes that human relationships to the earth can be lastingly successful only if fundamental ecological laws are respected. The "wooing of the earth" is possible if a relationship of re-spect and love, in contrast to exploitation for profit and power advantages, prevails.[16] He is quick to add that "the recycling of degraded environments is one of the most urgent tasks of our age." [17] It is in this reclaiming process that our security and our hope for the future resides.

Dubos stresses that as long as humanity continues to exist, it will intervene into nature. It must if it is to survive. But this must be done with a sense of responsibility for the welfare of the earth as well as for humankind. He says: "We must therefore attempt to anticipate the long-range consequences of our actions." [18] As we have seen, the extent of our intervention is influenced by social values and attitudes concerning natural resources. Quickly, we must learn of the value of diversity and flexibility in preference to narrow notions of efficiency, if our agriculture is to survive. Our future is durable only if it contains a great diversity in its complex symbiotic relationships.

These words of Dubos can be considered our basic challenge in agriculture. Dubos asks us to look for examples in such places as the diverse beauty of agriculture in the Loire Valley in France, the hedge-rowed farmlands of Cornwall and East Anglia in England, as well as the carefully preserved hillsides of Switzerland and Austria. In these significant instances, diversity and sustainability with justice have been established. The future holds promise.

But is this true of the farmlands on what used to be called "The Great American Desert"? Is this true of our gigantic irrigation systems of the corporate farms of the San Joaquin, Imperial, and Coachella Valleys of California, or over the Ogalalla Aquifer of Oklahoma, Texas, Colorado, or Wyoming? Are we making sure that at least 10 percent of every ecosystem remains in wilderness preserve, where the delicate edges of creation remain unmolested? What a challenge it is to talk about a preferred agriculture in the context of a vision of quality relationships on the one hand, and clarity of our present reality on the other!

I have lived through this challenge many times. One bright Sunday morning in the spring of 1977 in southern England, my wife and I decided to take a short trip into the countryside. We walked to the bus stop in our adopted village of Piddinghoe.

The village was built in the 12th century. It is perched picturesquely on the edge of the Sussex Downs. (Downs are rolling hills covered with pasture grasses and oak-lined ravines.) We walked down our graveled village road past the post office and pub. Beneath a great oak tree we waited for the bus. When we boarded it, we found ourselves among other picnicking families who were on their way to a favorite spot near the sea, where farmers pasture their sheep during the lambing season. Arriving at the village of Rottingdean, we followed the nearby trails, specifically designated for hiking and picnicking, onto the rolling fields. To everyone's delight, hundreds of ewes and lambs were grazing, nursing, and frolicking in the warm sunshine. To hear laughing children as they watched the joyful antics of newborn lambs was an added delight.

In previous centuries most of these hills were covered with brush and oak forests. Long ago, all of that vegetation had been cut for construction purposes and the making of charcoal. But, wisely, the people of the past century had launched programs to rehabilitate the badly eroded hillsides. Today, although the soil over these chalk hills is still thin, it is preserved and is slowly being built up by the root systems of the heavy pasture sod. The land is preserved for sheep grazing and for recreational purposes for the people of the nearby villages and the more distant cities. Because of the vast network of public transport, these magnificent hills are within easy and inexpensive reach of many people. There is no urban or industrial sprawl. New tax structures and inheritance laws, based on land permanently designated for agriculture, offer no threat to sheep growers. There are no dune buggies, recreational vehicles, or trail bikes. Instead, there are bicycle and walking paths, kite fliers, laughing children, nearby train stations, and convenient bus routes.

This experience—along with similar ones of justice and sustainability, beauty, harmony, and dignity that I have encountered in locations around the planet—inspire me, as they do Professor Dubos, with hope for a secure tomorrow for my own nation and for our global community of nations. Security and quality of relationships are found in these things.

A normative synthesis

A just, participatory, and sustainable agriculture will be one
in which people participate, directly and indirectly, in making
the decisions that affect them. It will be an agriculture in which
each one can feel secure that her or his quality of life will be
maintained at an acceptable level. The rate of use of nonrenewable resources used in its technologies will not outrun the
increase in resources made available through technological
innovation. The emissions of pollutants will be well below the
capacity of the earth to absorb them. With the meeting of these
basic needs people on the land will then be free to design and
pursue the development of greater quality in agriculture. Such
agriculture will develop quality in the relationships between
humankind and the resource base of the earth, both for the
well-being of the present as well as the future. These ideas
furnish us with a vision of how to invest in the land, express
our thanks for life, and secure hope for the future.

The vision of a preferred agriculture challenges us deeply.
Sustainability in our agriculture (and of our world) is a necessary and valid ethical imperative for political considerations
and for the ministry of the church.

If we attempt to put into practice the ethical perceptions
involving justice, participation, and sustainability which give
direction to the value base of coparticipation with God, then
the need to preserve the integrity of the natural world is clear.
It can be said that we and our descendants may live in this
world in dignity and beauty because it is God's world.[19] Freedom to use the environment ought to be restricted to ways that
are coherent and consistent with our perceptions of what God
wills for created life. From biblical perceptions we see that
humanity is not at the center of creation, but rather part of it.
Perhaps, at this moment of history, humankind is indeed at the
frontier of the evolutionary process. If so, then so are our
responsibilities and levels of accountability to participate in
the nurture of this evolution. Freedom to use the environment
ought to be restricted to these purposes and goals.

Richard Cartwright suggests that the needs of land-use systems must be represented in every decision-making process

concerning the land. That is, the environment itself must be formally represented within our ethical, legal, and constitutional system. Humanity is the conscious, sensory element in much of the ecosystem. The possibility for creative harmony, which enriches all, must be fulfilled. He suggests that the administration of the land should, in general, be in the hands of those who are closest and most dependent on it. He reminds us that redeeming the land and redeeming humanity are not separate tasks. Rather, they are interdependent. A sound land ethic will be based on a recognition of this interdependence between us and our environment, an interdependence which God established when God created us together.[20] In this light, society ought to understand ownership of agricultural land in terms of massive responsibility, in covenant, for its perpetual care. The society ought to assure agricultural landowners of their ability to carry out these endowed responsibilities.

This is quite an agenda for agriculture and for its essential supporting infrastructures. It is within this radically expanded context of awareness and being that we understand in greater depth the meaning of responsible freedom, its breadth as well as its limits.

PART 3

Toward Solution

> I can't myself raise the winds that might blow us, or
> this ship, into a better world. But I can at least put
> up this sail so that, when the wind comes, I can
> catch it.
>
> E. F. SCHUMACHER
> *Good Work*

7 Worldwide Solutions

There is no such thing as a simple solution to the complex set of problems related to the world food crisis. I have chosen to describe three areas of research and development for both U.S. and world agriculture that suggest how agriculture can begin the process of needed change in pursuit of a more preferred future. The synthesis of the purposes, technologies, and industries which these agricultural activities incorporate provide clues for ways to develop infrastructures for a more just, participatory, and sustainable agriculture. Each area points to the importance and urgency of moving forward with the research agenda of agriculture and of giving a high priority in the national budget to agricultural research and the development of new cropping systems.

Forest farming

The problem which J. Sholto Douglas and Robert A. de J. Hart address is stated in capsule form in the foreword written by E. F. Schumacher: "Civilized man has marched across the face of the earth and left a desert." [1] The authors expand this fundamental problem statement by saying:

> The most urgent task facing mankind today is to find a comprehensive solution to the problems of hunger and malnutrition, with all the disease and misery that they involve, by

methods that do not overburden stocks of renewable resources such as soil and minerals used for fertilizers, and do not impoverish the environment.[2]

These authors, and many others like them, are frustrated as they observe the level of ignorance about the function and potentiality of tree crops in the face of human dependence on a few cereals, annual legumes, tubers, and a few animals. They are deeply concerned about the hazards of existing agricultural technologies, of soil loss from the constant cultivation of annual crops, and from irresponsible animal-production activities that drain the world's grain supply. They are concerned about our vulnerability to drought, flood, and insect and disease pests. They are also concerned about the relatively few crops and our consequent thin thread of food security.

Douglas and Hart suggest that trees constitute one of humankind's most important assets and play a vital role in the maintenance of the global environment. Trees can play a significant role in overcoming the problem of worldwide food shortages, with accompanied agricultural-resource loss and environmental stress. Trees offer the possibility of far higher yields per acre of land than any other agricultural activity. The production and maintenance of trees and their products do not require costly and sophisticated technologies. Trees rehabilitate, preserve, and enhance soil resources. They maintain and improve water resources. They renew and preserve entire environments, involving the production of atmospheric oxygen, maintain balances of carbon dioxide, and provide stability in climatic patterns. Trees form the basis for the quality of human and animal life. Trees are the world's major fuel supply and a base for industry (in vegetable oils, clothing, construction, furniture making, and paper). Trees are highly tolerant of the variabilities of weather such as drought or flood.

One of the world's outstanding leaders in the promotion of trees and tree farming was Dr. Richard St. Barbe Baker. British-born in 1889, Dr. Baker has worked from the Sahara to the U.S. redwoods and from India to the Amazon. He was trained in France and Canada and earned his graduate degrees at Cambridge University in England in 1920. He served in Kenya, became the founding father of the international organization called "Men of the Trees," and helped design the Civilian Conservation Corps (CCC) for Franklin D. Roosevelt, a program employing six million persons in planting shelter belts from Canada to Texas. In 1930 he organized the purchase of 12,000 acres of California redwoods which later became a part of our national system of state parks. He initiated a shelter belt in Russia 3000 miles long, which employed more than 18,000,000 people over a 10-year period. He dispatched vast numbers of Scotch pine to China and helped Prime Minister Nehru begin reforestation in India. He was deeply involved in Sahelian reforestation and was an outspoken critic of deforestation activities in the Amazon. He reminded us all that of the 30 billion acres of land on the earth, more than 9 billion are already desert. He stressed that we could not afford to lose more of this green mantle, or the water tables of the continents would sink beyond recall. He stressed that trees are like the skin of the earth. If any being loses more than one-third of its skin, it dies. A country is very poor if it does not have trees.[3] He said this of the United States:

> This country is in a very serious position. The tree cover is very small and the desert is on the march. You have been wheat mining too long with big machinery and forcing the soil with chemical fertilizers. The soil is blowing away. You've got less than 20 years before a great part of your agricultural land will be desert.[4]

The importance of trees ought to be obvious. The development of their potential can be imagined as one is reminded that only 5% to 10% of the earth's surface is presently useful for production, three-fourths not being utilized for the production of food and fiber. Massive losses in vegetative cover and soil places the future in question. Tree farming is likely to increase food and fiber production three to four times that of present world production levels, a hopeful potential in view of present trends in population growth and resource consumption.

Douglas and Hart observe that there are two basic underutilized resources: human resources and the mineral-rich subsoil found in most of the places of the world that are presently too rocky or barren for conventional cropping systems. Any area receiving more than four inches of rainfall per year holds tremendous potential for the development of tree farming.

Centuries ago Buddha urged every person to plant and nurture at least one tree every five years. It is bewildering to contemplate what the surface of the earth would look like today and how the condition of humankind would be evaluated if everyone through the centuries from the time of Buddha would have followed this holy advice. Long before I had learned of Buddha's counsel, I made it a habit to plant somewhere an average of five trees per year, and to see to it, regardless of where I live, that they are nurtured toward maturity. I have urged others to do likewise.

Douglas and Hart remind the reader of the background of their research, which involved the work of the classic study done by J. Russell Smith, Emeritus Professor of Economic Geography at Columbia University. In 1929, Smith published his book *Tree Crops: A Permanent Agriculture.*[5] His thesis is that certain crop-yielding trees can provide useful substitutes for cereals in animal-feeding programs, while conserving the environment. He observed on the Mediterranean island of Corsica the large stands of chestnut trees which for centuries supported Corsican families. I have seen this same phenomenon in the highlands of Sicily. In the 1920s, Smith, like C. W. Lowdermilk, was working on the problem of overcoming famine in west China. There, he saw plowed treeless hillsides. Soil was irretrievably lost. He compared China with Corsica. One civilization was secure in the keeping of its trees; the other was destroyed by the spoilation of forests. Smith began to study this comparison. He developed the idea of incorporating trees into an integrated farming system. His vision: millions of green tree-covered hills, and nestling among them, thousands of farms and farm communities.

The Japanese evangelist Kagawa experimented with Smith's idea and founded the basis of the reforestation of Japan. In the process, he provided the basis for a new agriculture for those who were at that time poor, marginalized highland farmers. Many of Japan's forests were denuded for timber, fuel, furniture making, and shipbuilding. For poor people, the problem with the idea of conserving soil with trees was that there was no immediate economic return. People needed food and income immediately. So Kagawa organized large sections of the nation for planting walnuts and for feeding walnuts to pigs. This provided immediate cash income. Later, plantations of pine developed, which soon provided substantial income for highland people. The planned integration of economic tree species with commercial livestock emerged in time, and the idea of "three-dimensional farming" was born, which involved (1) conservation, (2) tree farming, and (3) livestock production.

Douglas and Hart began their experimental work in the 1950s in the Limpopo Valley just north of the Zoutspansberg hills in South Africa. They developed their work in collaboration with the International Commission for Applied Ecology, the World Academy of Arts and Sciences, and UNESCO. It involved the development of an area that was laid destitute from the conquest of the Matabele kingdom and the ensuing indiscriminate cutting and clearing of bush trees and shrubs. With a carefully planned program using two drought-resistant economic leguminous species of trees (the Algarroba or Mesquite) and the Carob *(Ceratonia siliqua)*, rehabilitation of the landscape and meaningful settlement of people took place. Many additional species have subsequently been planted and their products harvested.

Trees are important because of their vast variety and the possibility of enormous yields. Apples produce average yields of nearly seven tons per acre per year. The honey locust produces from 15 to 20 tons of beans and bean pods per year. This does not count what the yields can be if, beneath these kinds of trees, vines and vegetables are grown. These yields must be seen in comparison to average food and feed—grain yields of from $1\frac{1}{2}$ to 2 tons per acre annually.

Trees are able to develop deep taproots to reach underground water-bearing strata. Some penetrate several hundred feet into subsoil and rocky strata in search of moisture. When forests are either removed or planted, climates are modified. Before the shrubs and forests were cleared in the Mississippi basin, as much moisture was evaporated into the atmosphere from the transpiration of this vegetation than now goes out of the mouth of the Mississippi River every year.

Trees are of ultimate importance. When they are lost, so is lost the civilization that emerged out of their resource base. Now the problem is worldwide, and the future of our planet and all its inhabitants is threatened. Yet as critical as this subject is, we generally ignore it. In tree farming lies a partial answer to the question about food for tomorrow. Tree farming is a vital element in the model of sustainability in our food systems.

Douglas and Hart state their vision of tree farming:

> By means of forest farming, world production of foodstuffs and raw materials can be increased substantially and where appropriate, tree crops linked with industrial development; something of real significance will have been achieved . . . both for the better sustenance of mankind and for the preservation and enhancement of our environment.[6]

The aim of forest farming is to increase and diversify the productive capacity of woodlands so that, instead of only timber and related items, their output includes a wide range of foodstuffs and other raw materials. Agri-silviculture, in its broadest sense, defines all plant culture and livestock keeping as parts of one whole biological cycle, looking on each farm unit as a developing entity. Forestry is integrated with farming, animal husbandry, and horticulture to achieve both maximum output and optimum conservation of a given area.

When the system is fully in practice, it becomes three-dimensional: (1) sources of timber, conservers of the land against erosion, and assets for climatic amelioration; (2) harvests to nourish and fatten commercial types of livestock; and (3) animal products such as meat, milk, butter, cheese, and eggs. There are thus three benefits to be derived from this system of cropping, rather than the single one normally obtained from ordinary farming or forest exploitation. Added to these, a secondary output includes hides and skins, wool, honey from ancillary apiculture, gum, timber, charcoal, hay, and silage. This list is by no means exhaustive. In emergencies, the cereal substitutes produced by trees may be used for human food.[7]

Tree farming calls for the creation of large belts or blocks of economic trees interspersed with narrow grazing strips of grasses or herbage, along which move herds of livestock fed from the woodlands and producing meat and other items. The cereal substitutes harvested from the trees, supplemented by the pasturage, support the animals. The system forms a natural biological cycle into which humanity fits perfectly. We can eat the food harvested from the trees and the meat products of the forest-fed livestock. The manure of the animals is returned directly to the land, which encourages healthy and vigorous growth of plants. Agriculture of this type may be introduced in places where orthodox farming or forestry would be impractical or uneconomic. There are no expensive field operations or heavy capital outlays or machinery. Labor needs are very low, and, in general, the burden of work is lightened.

This three-dimensional concept has been designed to conform to ecological principles and practices. Each forest farm is intended to constitute a local ecosystem which has been imposed on a previously barren or unproductive area, or substituted for unprofitable existing agriculture or silvicultural holdings. The technique preserves and improves the ecology of regions. Its aim is to bring into being self-supporting units of production.[8]

Three-dimensional forestry achieves a synthesis of farming, tree growing, and animal husbandry. The three dimensions do not simply complement one another but become a single integrated whole. Unlike the medieval or traditional peasant methods of forest utilization, which were haphazard and unscientific, modern forest-farming activities are intensive and well planned. They have to be capable of adjusting to a wide variety of conditions according to the demands of specific environments.

Forest farming has the fundamental purpose of offering one complete and integrated applied science instead of the conventional separation of silviculture from agriculture, a cleavage which is unknown to nature. As we have noted, excessive specialization in agriculture and the dependence on monocultures have already inflicted great damage on different regions of the world by interfering with the ecological balance. Tree-cropping practices may redress to a considerable extent the obvious defects of orthodox farming and forestry which impede their effective use in areas where local conditions are too exacting for the extension of conventional methods. This possibility of forest farming in regions where ordinary cultural practices would stand no chance of success is important. Marginal lands occupy a high percentage of the earth's surface. At the present time, most of them are lying idle and derelict. The widespread introduction of tree crops will go a long way toward developing many currently useless jungles, moors, scrub savannas or thornbush, stony or sandy deserts, and what are so often ambiguously called "rough grazing areas." A further advantage of farming with trees is the general simplicity of operation, provided that broad principles are followed and proper methods applied.[9]

Forest farming requires further research. The most urgent problem is the comparative geographic study of the laws governing the natural associations of species formed in connection with farming systems. Today, these disturbed associations are either devoid of self-regulating mechanisms or they are generally weakened. A thorough investigation of various complexes of associations (agrocoenoses) will make it possible to determine the possibilities of influencing their formation purposively. Such investigations will also aid in outlining proper ways for applying agrotechnical and biological measures to achieve correct balance and active stimulation of useful species within an economic framework.[10]

In forestry today, the most advanced opinion contends that in creating a shelterbelt or a wood or forest for economic or ornamental purposes, humanity should conform as far as possible to the ecological conditions of the region. Forestation should be organized to approximate a region's natural ecological climax. To do this, a system of mutually interdependent associations of species needs to be formed which will be fully adapted to local soils and climatic conditions, while its constituent plants, as well as wildlife, would possess favorable relationships with each other.

A new environment would be created, with much of the diverse and abundant vitality of the primeval forest, with its natural checks and balances, its mechanisms of biological control, but consisting entirely of economic species carefully selected to perform single or multiple functions for the benefit of man.[11]

Douglas and Hart describe the design of a forest farm, its methodology, problems, and potentials of propagation and planting, and along with a discussion of leguminous, nut, forest, oil, and fodder trees. They apply these tree-crop categories to the ecosystem of temperate uplands and desert regions. In their book, they identify 126 species of browse plants and economically practical cover crops useful under forest plantings across a wide spectrum of soil and climate. They also identify 164 species of high-yielding grasses and herbage plants suitable for providing pasturage and extra fodder between and around trees on forest farms. Most species provide for the combined purpose of grazing, conservation, and reclamation. Most are perennial. Douglas and Hart have also comprised a unique listing of eight species (144 varieties) of oil-producing Eucalyptus appropriate for rather arid conditions.

Farm layout is designed around contours. Forests, woods, and orchards are interplanted with level grazing strips. There is an emphasis on the design of planting schemes employing canopy configurations, access roads, and fence lines for efficient field access and animal management.

Leguminous trees in many varieties can supply almost every nutritional need of humans and animals and are useful for commercial and industrial products. Leguminous tree products have equivalent nutritional potentials to fruits, nuts with protein equivalent to the best qualities of meat and fish, edible oils, and sugars. They have a wide climatic range. Most have a protein content ranging from 15% to 25%, as compared to 6% to 14% for the common cereals, but with added benefit of nitrogen fixation. *Leguminosae* are the second largest family of seed plants, containing some 600 genera with 13,000 species, and are cultivated throughout the world.[12]

Species of acacia (genus group of several hundred) have high-yielding products in the form of leaves, seeds, pods, gum, and bark. They do well on poor soil. The algaraba (*Prosopis* species) have many types that are more nutritious than corn, yielding something like beans, plus providing supplies of firewood, lumber, and a basis for honey. Bean-bearing pods appear within two years on many of the types. Roots extend to 100 feet for moisture, becoming drought resistant. Many yield two bean crops per year. The carob *(Ceratona siliqua)*, a native of the Mediterranean world and now worldwide, has valuable pods for humans and livestock, some yielding upwards to 1000 pounds per acre annually. They thrive on stony land in arid and semiarid regions. These trees produce food for one hundred years, some bearing up to 20 tons per year. The honey locust trees *(Gleditsia triacanthos)* are high producers in temperate regions, having the nutritional equivalent of prairie cereals. The list is long.

There are also many uses and potentialities for nut trees, including the almond, beech, brazil, bread nut, cashew, cheronji, chestnut, coconut, filbert, pecan, java, oak, pine, pistachio, walnut, and many more. All are of high food and feed quality, fulfilling the many functions of tree farming. All produce high yields. The same is true for fruit, oil, and fodder trees. Nut trees are useful for livestock feed, fuel, and fence posts. Thirty-one species and numerous varieties thrive over a wide range of ecological conditions.

The United Nations Development Program is at work all over the world on the rehabilitation of eroded watersheds, barren uplands, and deteriorated savanna lands. More than 200 million trees were planted between 1934 and 1943 in the Dakotas, Nebraska, Kansas, Texas, and Oklahoma. China has planted a shelterbelt 1000 kilometers long and 50 kilometers wide to stop encroachment of the Gobi desert. In Algeria a 1000-mile shelterbelt exists to contain the Sahara, built after the wars of colonial liberation from France. Similar efforts are under way in India. The need is widespread for planting in the Scottish moors, mid-Wales, the Pennine moors of Northern England, the highlands of Scotland, the Auvergene in France, the abandoned farmlands of Appalachia and Britain, and in the peat regions of Finland and Scotland. Trees used for such purposes include birch, Scotch pine, maple, horse chestnut, ash, hawthorn, crab, cherry, oak, holly, alder, poplar, willow, and cedar. All have various functions and are producers of food or fiber or fodder.

The value and potential of tree farming can hardly be overstated:

Civilizations have been born out of the immense fertility and wide power of satisfying human needs provided by forest conditions. Later, the same civilizations have succumbed to the devastation and erosion caused by excessive and uncontrolled tree felling, without provision for natural regeneration, and the sites of many ancient cities are now uninhabited deserts. Out of a wide-spread movement for the establishment of forest farms in many parts of the world, it is possible to envisage the establishment of new ecologically-based civilizations, more vital and more profoundly satisfying to all man's deepest needs than any known before.[13]

Grasses and shrubs

Not long ago, Dr. Wes Jackson, professor of plant genetics (now director of the Land Institute of Salina, Kansas), was driving through a relatively flat and prosperous Mennonite community in south central Kansas. During the previous night, the region had experienced a five-inch rainfall, not uncommon for that part of the Great Plains, a region of the world known for treacherous weather. Adjacent to the clean fence rows and well-kept houses and farm buildings were roadside ditches filled with soil runoff. For Jackson, this was yet a further example of the enormous loss of soil suffered throughout the history of agriculture, even in the region farmed by some of the most ethically and ecologically responsible farmers in the nation. Like the Amish of Pennsylvania, the Mennonites have a strong ethic of land stewardship. Yet the drainage ditches were full of muddy runoff.

It was at that moment in his life, after 45 years as a son of Kansas, alongside the field of one of the more responsible citizens of America, that Jackson began seeing that *agriculture is the problem*, rather than looking at agriculture as having some problems needing solution.[14] Although Jackson—like W. C. Lowdermilk, Aldo Leopold, and many others—had studied the history of agriculture, he suddenly perceived the reality that agriculture itself was the problem. It took me the best part of the same number of years, and then observing the United Nations Conference on Desertification, to come to the same conclusion.

Jackson's statement of the problem is the same as that of

the United Nations (as articulated in Nairobi in 1976), and as Douglas and Hart's—unprecedented soil loss places the future in severe question. In Jackson's part of Kansas, from 9 to 60 tons of soil per acre per year are lost, depending on the degree of land slope and the variability of weather. Jackson's operational thesis for overcoming the fundamental problem of agriculture (abusive technologies resulting in irrevocable loss) is the same as the central thesis of the concept of appropriate technology that emerged in Nairobi: that of approximating, with agriculture, the potentials of the productive capacity of the original biomass of a given ecosystem. For Jackson, an inhabitant of the semiarid prairie state of Kansas, appropriate technology does not develop around a hard winter wheat that was imported by German-speaking, Russian-born ancestors of the Mennonites, but rather around the original biomass of this region, herbaceous perennial polycultures: the grasses and shrubs that covered Jackson's part of the Great Plains during the past millennia, and which supported, over this same period of time, countless herds of animals.

Jackson rightly observes that nature tends toward a polyculture of perennials, while humankind tries to develop its agriculture in the opposite direction with monocultures of annual crops. Nature finds its relative stability in diversity. Humankind seeks its food security in uniformity. Jackson, like Dr. Okigbo of the International Institute of Tropical Agriculture, Ibadan, Nigeria, reminds us that of the thousands of seed-producing plant species, fewer than one percent have been utilized for food, clothing, and shelter. Less than a dozen provide the huge bulk of our food and livestock feed supply.

In nature, perennial polycultures (with a representation of annuals) provide their own reseeding, recycling of minerals, soil maintenance and soil building, maintenance of chemical and genetic diversity, and weed control. The whole system is fueled by the energy of the sun. No soil is lost in the process. On the contrary, soil slowly accumulates as in the deep deposits of Kansas, Illinois, Indiana, and Missouri.

In our monocultural agriculture since the time the human species settled into somewhat permanent communities, the opposite of nature's processes has unfolded. We provide for seed production and planting, for fertilizer, weeding with chemical and tractor power, soil preparation, chemical pest control, and plant breeding. These technologies are powered largely by fossilized fuel resources. Soil loss is incredibly high and irrevocable.

Jackson sees in this "split" (human ways from nature's way), the problem, yet at the same time, the direction toward solution. He calls for a "biological technical fix," using a term that might attract serious attention. He points to the vast potential in tree crops, but focuses on what he knows best: the potentialities of the herbaceous perennials which were indigenous to his homeland. This is another element of the model for a sustainable agriculture.

Jackson's group in Salina is working on the development of several of the hundreds of indigenous herbaceous perennials of the region. He refers to three for illustration—eastern gamma grass *(Tripsacum dactyloides)*, several relatives of the soybean *(Glycine max)*, and hog millet, of the *Panicum* complex.

The potentialities of these plants and many others hold as much promise now as did the once little-known perennial legume called the soybean, a plant which transformed vast acreages of the United States and now plays a massive role in international politics and trade. Almost no research has been done on the development of the crops and cropping systems now under study by this little group in Salina. Today our plant sciences are capable of developing the potentialities of many new prairie plants.

Jackson is quick to point to the benefits of herbaceous perennial polycultures. Since little to no tillage is necessary, fossil fuel can be conserved. A group of scientists from the University of Kentucky, reporting in *Science* (June 6, 1980), calculate that no-tillage agriculture is a vision which will be a clear reality by the end of this century. They predict that by the year 2000, as much as 65% of the acreage now in conventional crops will be in no-tillage. Because soil is continually covered with these perennials, soil is preserved and its fertility and structure enhanced. Few pesticides are required; the genetic reservoir is preserved and enhanced; the possibilities in the development of more nutritious livestock feed are expanded; and labor is saved.

Jackson describes what a new farming system and new farming communities can look like across the Great Plains, reflecting the normative concept of social justice and environmental and resource sustainability.[15] Within these relationships and structures, Jackson finds no conflict between high yields and sustainable cropping systems involving indigenous herbaceous perennials. With reference to the problem area of human taste for new foods, Jackson is optimistic. He writes:

> If only a hundredth of the advertising is applied to the promotion of eating these healthful grains that is applied to the array of unwholesome junk food we ingest now, no cultural barrier can stand in the way of their wholehearted adoption.[16]

The emergence of a national demand and support base for accelerating the kind of research and development required to give momentum to the kind of work Jackson's group represents is long overdue. The task ahead is to build the technological foundation and financial base for working toward this diversification of orientation and approaches. We also need facilities for the training of new generations of agricultural leaders who can contribute to the momentum which these efforts represent.

Indigenous livestock

David Hopcraft was born in 1937, a son of a cattle rancher in the Nakuru region of Kenya, East Africa. During his primary and secondary years of education he observed the increasing rate of soil and vegetative loss as a consequence of cattle rearing, be it careful ranching or traditional ranging. During these early years, he traveled extensively with his father into the interior regions of undisturbed ecosystems and noted the lack of environmental disturbance in the midst of vast populations of indigenous animals: eland, buffalo, wildebeest, kongoni, impala, gazelle, ostrich, and many other species. Both disturbed and inspired, he went on to do special work in zoology and botany at London University. Later, he went on to Berea College in the United States, and then, with a United Nations scholarship, he earned his Ph.D. at Cornell University in animal science and agronomy, specializing in wild animals and animal behavior and ecology. He was awarded his degree in 1975.

It was during a consultation session for the E. I. Lilly Endowment that I first made my acquaintance with Dr. Hopcraft. Since then I have had several opportunities to visit his ranch, located about 25 miles east of Nairobi on the high arid plains of Kenya.

The purpose of Hopcraft's work is articulated on the first page of his dissertation:

> Dedicated to the hope that man will wake up and cooperate with nature, in the knowledge that only then will nature continue to support life.[17]

Hopcraft points out that in Africa, as in many parts of the world, humanity has interfered with nature's balance. In most parts of Africa, humankind has decimated or exterminated the wild ungulate populations and has substituted cattle for them.

Once a section of the environment is changed, the rest naturally changes to the detriment of the ecosystem as a whole. Vegetational destruction and change take place, along with soil erosion. The overall effect of this process is twofold. First, water percolation into the soil is reduced, resulting in a lowered water table. Second, vegetational cover is reduced, causing the soil to heat during the hot days. This in turn increases the rising of hot air from the land surface, which pushes up moisture layers into the atmosphere. Rainfall is then reduced and winds increase. Water and wind erosion are inevitable; consequently, the productivity of these areas is reduced step by step. Today the end result is seen over much of Africa— drying-out conditions, advancing desert, and starvation.

Hopcraft rightfully claims that there exists an alternative to the destruction of Africa's rangeland. It is the simple act of living with the natural environment, instead of fighting or changing it in our blind effort to "improve" and to "progress." [18] So he asks:

Will African and other governments and peoples wake up in time, and cooperate with nature? Will we adapt a viable and highly productive system for the land, or will we continue to invest vast sums of money in destroying this amazingly complex, productive, but delicate system? [19]

On a ranch covering nearly 20,000 acres of arid short-grassed rangeland with a rainfall of between 15 and 30 inches, Hopcraft is engaged in a comparative study of productivity between well-managed Boron cattle, marginally-managed cattle, and one species of indigenous animals, the Thompson's gazelle. His research project was limited to this one species, though today one will find at least a dozen species of indigenous ungulates on the ranch. Careful studies over an extensive period of time were made on behavior (clan associations, territorial boundaries, population dynamics, variability in gestation patterns) and the effects of climatic and grassland conditions on these patterns. Although complex, the whole system added up to a pattern of delicate balance between behavior and the variability of productivity patterns of the grasses, shrubs, and trees. The patterns are fascinating.

The rate of productivity of meat production was astounding. In terms of lean meat produced per pound per acre, the gazelle reached 14.6; experimental Boron cattle under expert management, 7.9; cattle on well-managed stock farms averaged 3.9; and cattle under traditional stock-raising methods averaged one pound per acre. These figures for indigenous animal gains continue to climb. In terms of lean meat harvested, the gazelle produce about 47% of its live weight in carcass meat, in comparison to 32% for the best-managed Boron.

But the most important part of this research is in reference to the condition of rangelands being studied. Hopcraft observed that the cattle decimated the range, causing serious tracks, reducing vegetational cover, and upsetting vegetational climax. They were unable to produce as much in terms of edible products as even one species of gazelle under similar conditions. It became clear that reduction in vegetational cover occurs under the impact of cattle grazing.

The resulting imbalance of natural vegetative climax reduced productivity all the way round. The soil was compacted and grasses were trampled. This resulted in reduced water absorption into the soil. The soil rapidly became dry. In comparison, under experimental conditions using an indigenous animal species in this low-rainfall area, none of this damage occurred. As may be expected, nature-evolved species live in harmony with the environment. They do not damage it.

Furthermore, due mainly to the physiological and nutritional adaptions that fit them for living in these conditions, these animals proved considerably more efficient than cattle. A greater weight of meat was produced per acre, even though the cattle were under optimal management. Hides of far greater value were produced. Costs of management were considerably lower, as there were no dipping or innoculation costs. Watering costs were negligible, since the indigenous stock are efficient in body-temperature regulation and in recycling vegetative moisture in their systems. Hopcraft observes that wild ungulates make far more efficient use of the vegetation than cattle, and at the same time maintain vegetational balance biomass. He says:

> If one small species can do so much better than cattle, how much more efficient would be the usual ten to fifteen species found in these areas? Each lives in its own niche; together they utilize the whole vegetational complex evenly and completely. Thus, an over-all balance is perpetually maintained.[20]

Every time I visit this ranch, I think about how effectively desertification can be reversed with the combination of tree farming, the nurturing of restored grasslands, and the substitution for cattle and goats of the ungulates that are indigenous and so prolific in these regions. In this is rehabilitation, beauty, and food for tomorrow.

The birth of a new global agriculture

These illustrations of a new agriculture are different from present industrialized models in several obvious ways. They point to an integrated diversity of plants and animals in the cropping system. This is quite different from the present emphasis on capital- and chemical-intensive technologies for monocultural production. These three illustrations suggest

quite clearly the birth of a new global agriculture. Unfolding
in these illustrations is an intentional process of combining,
on a biologically sophisticated basis, the energies of the sun,
chemistry of the soil, vegetation, and animals to renew and
sustain these resources. The purpose is to develop with more
quality relationships of human life in the wide community of
created life, including, but certainly beyond, the interests of
human life. These illustrations express a reverence for life
and a demonstrated choice about responsibilities for the
future. They begin to define what is needed to achieve sustainable levels of production of food and fiber. They imply
diversification, decentralization, and a reversed migration of
people from the country to the city. They suggest new requirements for a strong social ethos about value and life-style, research, leadership, supportive economic structures, policy,
and law. They point to the substance and meaning of essential
infrastructure for a preferred agriculture.

8 U.S. Solutions

U.S. agriculture, like worldwide agriculture, needs solution. Agriculture is a massive problem. Its destructive record is written clearly across the face of the earth. Solution does not unfold in one place without having positive effects everywhere. Breakthrough in one place provides high expectations elsewhere. If U. S. agriculture can achieve an appreciable degree of sustainability, it will improve the chances of agriculture in many other places. U. S. agricultural science and technology are studied and transferred globally. The accomplishments of U. S. agriculture in reversing the destructive trends of agricultural resource loss and negative social environmental impact will likely be experienced globally in a relatively short period of time. So it is that in this global context we appreciate more fully the urgency for solution to the problem of U. S. agriculture.

The questions arise. Where do we find solutions? To what degree do proposals reflect biblical wisdom about our relation to creation and covenant in the contemporary world? Ecologically, how can agriculture be shaped so that the interdependencies of the natural order—the elemental preconditions for life —can be maintained? How can U. S. agriculture achieve a quality of relationship to the earth in the present and future? How is reverence for the gift of life expressed in agriculture?

Problem awareness

The problem of the world agricultural crisis, with a focus on the crisis of U. S. agriculture, has been described at length in Part 1. What remains to be said is that the first steps toward the solution of any problem are in the clarification of its magnitude, causes, and consequences. The human species is different from a stampeding herd of cattle headed for a cliff. We are capable of reversing our direction. We are able to change our values and technologies if we see that the consequences are disastrous. As evidenced by the contemporary literature in the field of agriculture and in federal, state, and international documents, the problem of agriculture, and U. S. agriculture, is being defined adequately. The consequences of this "collision course" are predictable. The first responsibility for all of us in pursuit of solutions to U. S. agriculture is to broaden the social awareness of the problem to the extent necessary to initiate the process of technological and policy development to make needed changes. This work must take place throughout our educational institutions and the media. The process must take place in our social, economic, and political debates—from town meetings to Congress, and from the village drugstore to the corporate boardroom.

The vision of a preferred future

Erik P. Eckholm concludes his latest book in recognition of the tenth anniversary of the Stockholm Conference on the Human Environment by saying: "Environmental choices must be guided by a vision of a desirable human society and the quality of the natural environment needed to support that vision." [1] Likewise, choices about agriculture must be guided by a vision of a desirable human society and the quality of relation to the earth. In view of this truth I labor to articulate an ethic, vision, and goal of a just, participatory, and sustainable agriculture. I have tried to determine the correlation between this ethic, goal, and vision, and biblical wisdom about creation, life, gift, and covenant. The ideas are universal. They are tested by history. They are ecologically sound. They point to a desirable vision of human society and quality relationships to the earth.

The vision reflects an informed ethical construct for making intentional and enlightened choices in the process of reaching solution to the problem of U. S. agriculture.

Technological and policy development

Technological development.   In *Beyond the Age of Waste,* a report to the Club of Rome by Dennis D. Gabor and Umberto U. Colombo, a startling fact is cited: "Research remains one of the weakest links in agricultural development. Today, investments in agriculture represent 0.25% of the GNP of the affluent nations, and between 1% and 2% of the GNP of the food-deficit nations." [2]

S. H. Wittwer, director of the Michigan State University Agricultural Experiment Station at East Lansing, gives further insight into these statistics. He points out that productivity of food crops has plateaued. Yields in wheat, maize, soybeans, and potatoes have not increased since 1970. Increases in world gains in food production are a result of the expansion of land under cultivation, not from the intensification of cropping systems. Yields rose after World War II due to those technologies which required massive inputs of fossil energy, fertilizer, pesticides, irrigation, mechanization, and new seed. Wittwer points out that now all these inputs except genetic development are increasingly subject to the constraints of cost, nonrenewable resource exhaustion, soil loss, and the dramatic reduction of organic matter in our soils.

In the face of all these things, there has been nearly a 15-year erosion of federal investments in agricultural research. The student enrollment in the land-grant universities and colleges of agriculture has tripled during this same 15-year period of time, with little increase in faculty to accommodate this heavier teaching load. Classroom instruction has been met at the expense of research. Research has been left waiting, research to assure stability in our cropping systems and the development of nonpolluting technologies. Wittwer points out that it takes more than five years to get this kind of research going. [3]

Reflecting the suggested agricultural research agenda of the Research Council of the National Academy of Sciences, Wittwer articulates the agenda for the development of the resource base for a preferred agriculture: greater photosynthesis efficiency, improved biological nitrogen fixation, new techniques for plant and animal genetic improvement, more efficient nutrient and water uptake and utilization, reduced losses of nitrogen fertilizer from nitrification and denitrification, and more resistance to competing biological systems and environmental stress tolerances.[4]

The assumption behind all these activities is that new technologies would be economically, socially, and ecologically sound. Such technologies have the potential of making the transition from a nonrenewable to a renewable resource base in agricultural production.

Dennis Gabor and Umberto Colombo expand this agenda by suggesting research priorities for better utilization of soil and grass resources by animals, genetic development of efficiency in plant use of solar energy, more continuous cover crops, new nitrogen-fixing crops, improved energy ratios in food production, development of nonconventional high-protein food commodities, integrated pest control, the development of better uses for low-grade phosphate rock, more ecologically adaptable rotation systems, and agrarian reform with improved social policy about agriculture.[5]

In his paper "New Grants Program in Agriculture," Gary A. Strobel expands this agenda by pointing to the need for more research in alternative energy sources, forestry development, the rebuilding of the nation's farm extension service, improvement in animal health, improved utilization of our organic wastes, and better marketing systems. Like the others, he calls for substantial grants for the research of nitrogen fixation, photosynthesis, biological stress tolerances of plants and animals, and expanded work in plant genetics—all focused on improving plant and animal disease resistance, lessening the need for pesticides, and optimizing legume-rhizobium interactions for greater nitrogen fixation.[6]

Dr. Bede N. Okigbo, the assistant director of the International Institute of Tropical Agriculture (IITA) of Ibadan, Nigeria, offers an astonishing list of plant materials that illustrates the massive and largely untouched resource base for the development of a preferred agriculture.[7] He notes that of about 350,000 species of plants:

1. 10,000-20,000 can be broadly classified as cultivated for various purposes.
2. Not more than 10,000 fit into man's economic activities.
3. At least 3,000 species are grown for food.
4. 100 to 150 species are of major commercial importance.
5. Only 15 species contributed to the bulk of man's food.
6. The 14 most important food crops consist of six grasses: rice, wheat, corn, barley, sorghum, sugar cane; three roots and tubers: potato, sweet potato, cassava; three legumes: soybeans, common beans, groundnut; and two fruits: coconut and banana.

Okigbo points out that about 30% of humanity's energy comes from one grass (rice), and 70% of human food comes from one or more grasses. He also stresses that many of the highly commercialized crops have become so dependent on human inputs that they can hardly survive in nature. Moreover, not only has the number of cultivated plants and other plants used by the human species continued to decrease, but modern plant-breeding techniques and processing for convenience foods has further reduced the number of species in our diet and increased uniformity within each species. In some crops the uniformity has reached such a state that concern about their narrow genetic base and vulnerability to disease and pests has led to the present interest in maintaining large collections of useful germ plasma and increased plant-exploration activities.

Okigbo indicates that under present international study are 35 leafy vegetable species, 122 fruits and seeds, and 30 starchy roots and tubers—all having high potential. Okigbo lists over 90 plants of tropical Africa alone which are not receiving the attention they deserve. He says: "There is as much need to establish plant collectives as there is to increase the range of food crops under active study and regular cultivation."[8]

Substantial hope for achieving a sustainable agriculture is based on the research and development of these existing plant species. Many agricultural activities are substantially unfolding in the applied research of these combinations of plants, but we have a long way to go.

As we have seen in this chapter, the reforms needed by U. S. agriculture are possible to achieve, at least technologically. The question remains: Can we generate the social will to achieve the needed reforms? I believe that we can. My hope lies in the religious tradition of our culture. There is a general willingness to be responsible in relationship to the land, particularly when we are aware of the problem and have a vision of a better future.

Policy development.   In his book *Farmland or Wasteland,* R. Neil Sampson, executive vice-president of the National Association of Conservation Districts, suggests that we must look at three levels of policy and reform if we are to overcome our accelerating direction toward massive upheaval and loss in U. S. agriculture by the end of this century and if we are to achieve a sustainable future.[9] I find his suggestions helpful in clearly identifying what needs to be done.

1. Policies for *short-term* reform over a period of 10 years must address the need to reduce topsoil erosion, limit the conversion of prime agricultural lands for nonagricultural purposes, carefully develop remaining soil and water resources, and work for efficiency in land use in relation to urban growth.

2. *Mid-term* policies, which cover a period of 20 to 50 years, call for expanding efforts in crop and livestock research for sustainability along the lines illustrated in Chapter 7 and in the preceding section of this chapter, with reference to efficiency in crop production and harvest, storage, processing, preparation, distribution, and in the development of more nutritious foods.

3. *Long-range* policies for achieving a sustainable future in agriculture involve periods of more than 50 years. The needed reform is in integrating production costs into commodity prices which reflect costs of resource protection, strengthening farmers' capacities to innovate without abusing the soil or ruining landscapes. Reform is also needed to maintain international

trade in agricultural commodities and, at the same time, maintain sustainability in the production process.

I have found these three policy categories helpful. They clarify priorities of concern and action sequences. They give direction to needed technological research, development, and social change. They give realism to our expectations of how long it will take to achieve the goals of a preferred agriculture. These categories point to the interrelationships of farmland preservation; soil conservation; fertility maintenance, research, and development for a sustainable agriculture; and the integration of production costs into commodity prices and the emergence of new structures of international trade in agricultural commodities.

The research and development agenda has been identified for several years. The task is immense and will require massive state and federal funding. Businesses and industries associated with agriculture must also share in this responsibility. The magnitude of soil abuse has been described. The fact that 12 square miles of prime farmland go out of production each day for other purposes (a one million acre per year loss of primeland in addition to two million acres of rangeland loss) has been documented. Our first priority is to find solutions to this problem. The hope for taking further steps in research and development for a preferred agriculture is found in meeting the immediate need of dealing with the loss of farmland. It is important to discuss this point more fully.

Following the publication of the final report of the National Agricultural Lands Study in 1981, a reference book on the protection of farmland was published in 1982.[10] This work is the first of its kind in our nation's history. The authors searched the United States, drawing lessons from 18 case studies of state and local programs in farmland preservation. These experiments are located in Virginia, New York, California, Colorado, Oregon, Iowa, Pennsylvania, Minnesota, Wisconsin, South Dakota, Maryland, and Hawaii. It is interesting to learn that the history of American activities to preserve farmland is so recent. The story begins in Maryland in 1956 with efforts to reduce tax burdens on farmers. During the past 28 years, creative experiments in protecting farmers and farmlands have taken place, though most actively unfolding following the war in Vietnam. Of the 18 programs reviewed in the National Agricultural Lands Study, all but two were created after 1970 (Hawaii's land use law of 1961 and California's Williamson Act of 1965).

Eight types of responses have been given to alleviate crisis of farmland loss due to the pressure of the growth of suburbs, the interstate highway system, water development projects, extensive surface mining, and industrial sprawl (23.4 million acres lost in the eight-year period from 1967 to 1975).[11] They are: tax relief incentives (differential assessments, property tax credits, death tax benefits to farmers), agricultural districting, right-to-farm legislation, agricultural zoning, purchase and transfer of development rights, land-use controls, metropolitan growth-management programs, and integrated state programs of incentives and control. These programs have had their successes and failures. Each is complex in design and administration. In every case, attempts have been made to enable farmers to continue farming by protecting both the attractiveness of farming as a way of life and its profitability. Land development regulations and incentives deal only with a part of the overall problem and have been developed to meet various legal and constitutional requirements. They have been based on sound legislation and developed through comprehensive planning and policies which give appropriate recognition to low- and moderate-income housing, commerial and industrial development, and environmental protection objectives. At the same time, they have sought to safeguard private property by due process, equal protection, and adherence to the United States Constitution. Activity is growing in these response options and gives some indication of hope for the future. Land banking by state and federal government has yet to be initiated in the United States, even though this approach is being used with varying degrees of success in Western Europe.[12]

The critical need is to find places for the nation's expanding and mobile populations to live and work. The National Agricultural Lands Study on *The Protection of Farmland* emphasizes the finding that unless growth can be managed so that needed urban, industrial, and recreational development is provided in locations that do not threaten agriculture, efforts to protect agricultural lands will not be effective for long. Programs to protect land for the long run represent fundamental social decisions. Therefore, they should be developed in a comprehensive planning context, taking into account the community's need for land for industry and commerce and for residences for people of all social and income classes.[13]

A central conclusion can be drawn: urban growth boundaries need to be defined in ways that clearly separate areas in which agriculture is to be regarded as a long-term activity. In so doing, geographic and policy frameworks can be constructed to protect agricultural land and provide realistic expectations for landowners and developers. One of the many recommendations offered in this study is that states should provide leadership and programs for saving farmland. They need to be based on accurate information about the realities and trends in farmland use. Able and dedicated political leadership is essential. Obviously, much more than land-use controls and tax incentives are required to bring farmland preservation into reality. All efforts must be designed with every safeguard accorded to private property by the law.

Only when farmland is preserved is it possible to ease the problems of soil erosion and fertility loss. The same is true in terms of making sustainable technological innovations for a sustainable agriculture. Only when farmland prices are within financial reach of young farmers can new generations move to the land and make secure domestic food supplies.

Implications

The implications of these three approaches to U.S. solutions are awesome.

1. A massive educational effort must be undertaken to bring to the attention of the citizens of this nation the magnitude of the problem we face and what is required to solve it. Associated with this effort is the building of adequate state and federal budgets for doing the required research for a sustainable agriculture and the support of public policies that will safeguard

the nation's prime agricultural farmland for generations to come. This educational process should be a part of the social studies programs in our public and private schools, colleges, and universities, and in the production of audiovisual presentations in our news media. Such efforts must be felt in legislative activities of the states and in the houses of Congress.

2. Implied in the entire discussion about solutions to U.S. agriculture is the need for a social maturity and responsibility of land ownership. Biblical wisdom shows that land is a gift and that we relate to it with a clear understanding of stewardship and accountability to the present and the future. Land ownership has both its rights and its duties. We can see these responsibilities in our time, now that the frontier days of endless resources are history, and we find ourselves living in a world of limits.

3. To move beyond our crisis to a sustainable future in agriculture, several implications about agricultural structures are clear. There is a need to move from large-scale agribusiness enterprises to the development of skilled family farm operations, from the vertical integration of production through marketing and distribution to regionalization and efficiency in energy uses in distribution and processing, and from a capital and chemical-intensive technology to one that is biologically intensive as a consequence of a personal management of our many microenvironments. We are called to think about agricultural efficiency, not in terms of the maximization of yields per acre, but in terms of sustainable (regenerative) yields within the capacity of a given environment with its unique resource base. Implied in much that has been said is the fact that policies for the provision of cheap food must give way to agricultural commodity price structures which reflect sustainable costs of production and the provision for secure lives of the nation's farmers and rural communities. To solve the crisis we have to think in long-range time frames rather than immediate cost/benefit terms.

4. Implied in the quest for a sustainable, just, and participatory agriculture is the need for a redefinition of agricultural education and where it takes place. The land grant college establishment (research, extension, education) has to broaden

its emphasis to include the study of values and ethics, purposes and goals. The need to broaden the emphasis on crop production to the many other dimensions of the agricultural complex has been identified throughout this book. Research has to address the issues of atmospheric deterioration and postpetroleum technologies and questions of food quality and primeland preservation with appropriate social policy. Perhaps our colleges of agriculture ought to be called "schools of landscape management." Certainly agriculture ought to be studied comprehensively in every liberal arts college, in programs in social and political science, business management, economics, and social philosophy. If not, how can we expect knowledgeable, sensitive, and imaginative leaders in government, science, and business who can deal with agriculture in responsible ways?

5. Implied in what has been suggested in directions for solution to the U.S. agricultural crisis is a new understanding about the locus of domestic and international food security. Two issues are clear. First, food security is found in the farming sector of the nation's citizens. There is little hope in our food production system when between 3% and 4% of the nation's citizens are farming, while the remaining 96% to 97% of the people are dependent on this small number. In terms of the careful management of the nation's vast agricultural resources and the development of a diverse and integrated agriculture, large numbers of skilled and secure people are needed.

With reference to global food-security systems, no nation will achieve its essential goal of a sustainable, self-reliant food system if it continues to play the international game of comparative advantage in agricultural commodity imports and exports, the rules having been established during the colonial period of the past 200 years.

6. Essential for the achievement of a sustainable agriculture is the redevelopment of rural America: its towns and villages, schools, religious institutions, health services, and cultural amenities. The rural migration and consequent urbanization which this country has experienced since the end of World War II must end and reverse itself. The task will be monumental.

7. If agriculture is to be made secure and quality in relation-

ships to the land restored, then constitutional amendments will have to be devised to protect the environment and national resource base. During the early days of the formation of this nation and its Constitution, the issues involved in resource protection and the rights of all forms of life were beyond imagination. Today, however, we are able to see more clearly the importance of recognizing and dealing with these matters, for we now know the meaning of limits and the necessity for environmental preservation.

8. Finally, implied in the solutions to U.S. agriculture is the need for the nation's citizens to make a dramatic shift from the "now generation" mentality to one that values the prospects of a quality future for those who will follow. This requires maturation in value orientations and growth in moral development. Without such value perceptions and commitments, it is difficult to predict whether or not there will be food for tomorrow.

In conclusion, it is useful to return to Wes Jackson's question: "Is it possible that we simply lack enough stretch of our ethical potential to evolve a set of values capable of promoting a sustainable agriculture?" It seems to me that we have the technological potential to achieve the goal. But do we have sufficient will? My reply to Jackson's question is affirmative.

The mainstream biblical traditions concerning our relationship to the land run deep in our nation. When we are aware, we are offended by the realities of soil abuse and agricultural land loss. It seems to me that being offended reflects our religious understanding about what is right and wrong in our relation to the land. We "feel" the ecology of God, creation, and humanity. This is to say, we sense the interconnectedness of things and appreciate the fact that the land is God's gift and that we have accepted it in covenant.

The ideals of justice and righteousness in the whole fiber of creation are not new. We resonate to the poetry of the psalms and the prophets. We understand the truths in Rom. 12:1-2.

> I appeal to you therefore, brethren, by the mercies of God, to present your bodies as a living sacrifice, holy and acceptable to God, which is your spiritual worship. Do not be conformed to this world but be transformed by the renewal of your mind,

that you may prove what is the will of God, what is good and acceptable and perfect.

In place of conformity to the status quo, these verses point us to the promise of all things made new.

The ideas of justice, participation, and sustainability do indeed stretch our ethical potential and challenge us to work for a preferred future in agriculture. We understand that the future of agriculture is basic to everything else, including the course of human history. In biblical wisdom we have ethical standards for evaluating agriculture and for envisioning new directions for it. We have the ethical as well as technological base for generating the social will to create and implement the immediate, medium-, and long-range policies and reforms essential for the solution to the problem of United States agriculture and for guaranteeing the future of agriculture, both nationally and globally.

9 The Tasks of the Church

The outcome of human history will be determined by our resolve to achieve a preferred future for agriculture that has been advocated in this book. But can the history of agriculture be reversed? The underlying assumption is that it can. However, this depends on a shift from relating to the sustaining resources of the created world as objects for exploitation to seeing the resources of the earth as subjects of God's orderly creation and purpose. The problem of agriculture, domestic or international, is a profoundly spiritual matter. Working for the solution is a fundamental responsibility of the churches.

The issue context of the churches in review

As we saw in Chapter 5, "Ancient Wisdom for New Problems," the biblical world view, like the new frontiers of biology and physics, understands the interdependencies of all of creation— the interdependencies of elemental preconditions essential for life and its continuation. The key to the future is to understand and preserve these relationships rather than to learn how to get the most out of its parts.

The Old Testament stresses the point that humanity has no preeminent position. The human species is part of the order of creation—not set apart, above, or beyond it. Humanity is not exempt from responsibility for the created order. Rather, all life unfolds for the sake of the whole of creation. In biblical wisdom, the human species is endowed with a greater responsibility, that of participating in the creative process. We have a unique task: to guarantee the quality and the integrity of these life relationships for the purpose of keeping the creative process alive and moving—to establish a full justice that reflects cosmic order.

The New Testament experience empowers us with a new orientation and life to meet these challenges. In Christ our lives take on a new quality of relationship as part of the kingdom of God. In Christ there is a transformed perspective directed toward all sectors of life and the elemental guarantees of the natural world. The New Testament calls us to see the world and its future in the light of redemption in Christ. We see the world as God's world, not ours.

This faith and experience transform our self-centeredness and make change in the course of agricultural history possible. All things are made new. Life is wrested from death; the impossible becomes possible.

Biblical wisdom furnishes us with a foundation for building an ethic for a new agriculture—one based on justice, participation, and sustainability. This ethic includes human concerns, but moves beyond to a concern for all life and life-support patterns in the whole order of God's creation. The essence of this is integrity, beauty, and harmony of relationships between humankind and the earth, in the future as well as in the present.

With this orientation to agriculture, each one of us can feel secure that the quality of life expressed in God's creation will be maintained. As discussed in Chapter 6, the rate of use of nonrenewable resources in agricultural technology will not outrun the increases in resources made available through technological innovations. The emissions of pollutants will not exceed the capacity of the earth to absorb them. Agricultural technologies will develop within the limits of renewable resources. Agriculture will contribute to the maintenance of the diversity and interconnectedness of this diversity within nature. Agriculture will engineer quality in the relationships between humankind and the resource base of the earth, both for the well-being of the present and the future.

The program for achieving a preferred agriculture is vast and far-reaching. It is probably the most critically important item on the agenda of every nation in the international community. The concepts which have a chance of correcting the long and destructive course of history require changes in legal frameworks and social attitudes in order to design new technologies and social and economic structures for resolving our present complex problems of relationship with the creation. This requires expanded theories of value, new understandings about relationships and policies, and new laws and regulations for the purpose of maintaining the integrity of the ecosystem of planet earth. Environmental and resource issues and land-use questions need to be represented in our ethical, legal, and constitutional system and in our structures of law and law enforcement. The interdependence of God's established order of creation must be maintained. Society must be structured in such a way that it will help those on the land to fulfill their special responsibilities of stewardship on behalf of us all and of the future.

As discussed in Chapter 8, the task is twofold. The first is the technological development of farming systems that are coherent and consistent with the ideals incorporated in the biblical wisdom of relationships and purposes, time and process. This requires the invention of new models of farming which approximate the productivity of the biomass of the original biotic community and its resource base. The second task is in the development of policies and their implementation for essential reform in law and custom that make the preservation of farmland and new agricultural systems possible and give essential social and economic support to those who farm the land.

The tasks

We understand the context and the problem of agriculture. We have biblical perspectives that help us develop a new ethic of agriculture. Now the question is: What are the tasks of the churches in implementing this new ethic? Involvement in hard work and long reflection across a wide spectrum of effort in more than 50 nations has helped me identify four major tasks for the churches.

1. Responsible freedom and liberation

The Christian faith enables us to see beyond immediate human needs to a concern for all of life. We cannot hope for the emergence of a new agriculture—one that is just, participatory, and sustainable—until we break through the restrictions of our narrow human-centeredness which causes us to see the world and its resources as objects for exploitation for meeting immediate human needs. Biblical insights enable the human species to transcend these propensities and ask the question first and foremost: What is God's will for all of life and our relation to it? The first task of the church is to instill this question into the center of the decision-making process of the society and its understanding of order. A theocentrism leads to a biocentrism and consequently to a whole new perception about the limits and potentialities of agriculture. Freedom then becomes responsible because it is tinged with the idea of accountability to God's will for the creation. Responsible freedom becomes an expression of covenant, and covenant is seen as an expression of partnership.

With this notion of responsible freedom, the church liberates people from the restrictions of social, economic, and technological tradition and conventional morality. In this freedom, people are liberated from their fears of ridicule and isolation which are the inevitable consequences of innovation felt by those in the rural setting and in the land grant colleges whose faculty and staff live within the restrictions of an agricultural science and technology of limited time perceptions, interest, and purpose. Until this liberation takes place, changes in the course toward a more just, participatory, and sustainable agriculture do not occur.

We can remember Jesus' sermon in the synagogue at Nazareth in which he quoted Isaiah: ". . . to set at liberty those who are oppressed and to proclaim the acceptable year of the Lord" (Luke 4:18-19). In this spirit, the role of the church is to enable this kind of liberation to take effect in the lives and places of service of those members who struggle to take initiatives for a more preferable agriculture. This struggle involves farmers, teachers, research workers, and rural community leaders who have committed their lives to strengthening the nation's agricultural support structures. The church's support should be felt by those people who find themselves isolated by their peers because of their efforts to address the problem of agriculture in our time and place.

2. Prophetic witness

The second task of the church is to witness prophetically to the problem of American agriculture. When one lives through the statistics of Part 1, one feels like Jesus confronting the money changers in the temple! One of the leading reasons for the design of the first part of the book is to suggest the dimension, need, and urgency for this kind of witness. The churches have a strong record of helping the nation address such issues as clean air, clean water, civil rights, arms expenditures, nuclear warfare, and world hunger. They must likewise take up responsibility for addressing the problem of American agriculture.

3. Envisioning

The third task of the church is to envision a preferred agriculture for a preferred future. Chapters 7 and 8 made suggestions about the nature of this vision. The task is to speak positively of the challenge and its potential. We all know that addressing the vision of a preferred agriculture requires depth in understanding. This task is not easy, because only fragments of new models exist, and we do not have historical precedents of any real significance to help us. However, if the normative ideas are kept in focus (the idea of a just, participatory, and sustainable agriculture), then the search, identification, and articulation of models approximating these criteria are manageable.

The church has an established precedent in this envisioning process. It is found in the Lord's Prayer, which speaks of God's will being done on earth as it is in heaven. The Old Testament concepts about order and creation (justice and righteousness) which have been identified as illustrations in Chapter 5 provide substance for this vision. One of the purposes of Chapter 7, with reference to forest farming, the use of perennial grasses, shrubs, and indigenous livestock, is to make concrete suggestions for envisioning. A new ethic for a new agriculture, with suggestions for immediate, mid-range, and long-range strategies in U.S. agriculture, has been presented in Chapter 8 as means for giving direction and meaning to this envisioning process.

4. Leadership nurture for model building
The churches can nurture the development of models of a preferred agriculture. The churches must address the problem of U.S. agriculture and the question about food for tomorrow in worship, teaching, and preaching; in community, youth, and adult activities; in centers of administrative and spiritual authority; and in structures of outreach in mission, life, and work in the seminaries and publishing houses. The concern for the food and the agricultural problem, for today and tomorrow, needs to be nurtured in the lives of leadership—clergy, academic, agricultural-industrial workers, farmers, agribusiness management, and throughout the whole spectrum of the agricultural and rural community infrastructure. Workshops, seminars, and regional consultations of every kind need to be conducted in pursuit of action opportunities for everyone.

Creative confrontation, stimulation, and the support of concerned people need to be strengthened in the ministry of the churches. The ministry of the church must be felt in the development of a social sensitivity to the problem and the possibility of agriculture. Then this sensitivity must be expressed in social demand for policy, law enforcement, and evaluation of how we use the land, to see that what happens to land is consistent with the vision of a just, participatory, and sustainable agriculture. The church must ask the land-grant colleges for accountability to normative understandings of agriculture, society, and the future. Because agricultural training takes place only in the state colleges and universities, this responsibility of the church exists. Hopefully, private colleges and universities will begin to bring agricultural issues into their curriculum.

These tasks of the churches in U.S. agriculture are a challenge. But this is not the first time in history that the church has been confronted with a challenge. This simply illustrates once again the deeper meanings of discipleship and salvation.

Time is long overdue for the churches, in their many denominational forms, to consider how they are organized to provide responsible ministry to their rural constituencies as well as to the nation. The churches need to listen to the concerns of rural congregations. In ecumenical cooperation, the denominations need to take up specific responsibilities for program assistance for addressing the many critical issues in rural America today. The denominations need to create opportunities for dialog between rural and nonrural people about our common concerns. Assistance needs to be given in linking knowledgeable persons and agencies who can help the churches address local, national, and international structures that negatively impact rural communities and the land. The denominations must organize themselves to communicate information, to provide educational opportunities and advocacy efforts concerning rural issues and ministry to all congregations, and to create specific rural ministry networks of support and concern. The denominations should be actively engaged in providing special services for rural congregations and clusters of congregations in response to their requests for assistance. Consultations and conferences on local, regional, and national levels need to be convened to pursue the growing awareness of need to strengthen the church's ability to respond to the kinds of tasks outlined above.

All of these tasks and issues of concern need to be addressed in theological education and programs in continuing education for church leaders. Traditions in biblical study and exegesis need to be reexamined in light of the agricultural issue context of the churches in rural ministry. For example, have we interpreted biblical literature in ways that are self-serving, or do we understand the full meaning of servanthood in terms of our relationships and responsibilities to the whole creation? Likewise, assumptions need to be questioned in the fields of church history, ethics, and theology. Are our orientations inclusive of the whole history of creation and our relation to it, or are they narrowly focused on the human experience and perspective? The implications of the tasks of the churches working for the achievement of a preferred agriculture are awesome.

A forgotten dimension of ministry

How can the churches even begin to feel as though they can accept the tremendous responsibility for taking up its agenda? Walter Brueggemann gives us a clue.[1] He appreciates the awesome responsibilities of Christian witness and service in our time of massive power complexes and a changed role in ministry. He suggests that the biblical model of the "wise man" is appropriate to ponder seriously, even taking precedent over our more common notion of ministry in priestly and prophetic forms. Brueggemann helps us see that in the Bible the wise man was the confidant to the powerful people (kings and queens, governors and generals). These wise people made few claims for themselves, but did stand in strategic positions to put forth the right kinds of questions or to make the right kinds of observations to significantly affect policy and action.

In this sense our purpose as Christian leaders is to enable needs to be felt. People of power (whether corporate executives or affluent folk seeking safe investments in the land) need "question-putters" who can probe larger visions so that power does not lead to endless cycles of acquiring more power. Wise people have to ask questions about hidden issues, relationships, options, and about private and communal good, including not only the present but the future.

It is unfortunate that, most of the time, people of power are burdened with their own immediate set of responsibilities. They do not have time for the luxury of pondering questions of meaning or long-range consequences. But, as Brueggemann puts it, "Ministry has the opportunity and responsibility to be at the right place at the right time with compelling vision and the appropriate question for reflection." [2] This function is critically important when we ask the question: "Will there be food for tomorrow?"

The wise person has the ability to put questions of meaning in ways that enable people of power to discover insights as their own. The wise person helps the powerful to probe for options and to explore the limits beyond which power results in life rather than death. The wise person encourages the "kings and queens" to feel the need for a better perspective.

Within this role of ministry, neglected in the contemporary American church, it is easy to find oneself on the margin of things rather than front and center. It leaves one without conventional identity, conventional support, or job description. In many ways, it is to those on this "margin of ministry" that this book is addressed, in a spirit of hope.

Notes

Chapter 1

1. Walter Ebeling in *The Fruited Plain* (Berkeley: University of California Press, 1976), p. 317, makes the following comparison: If the world were reduced to the size of a billiard ball, mountains would not be seen and the surface would appear to be smooth.
2. John A. Livingston, *One Cosmic Instant: Man's Fleeting Supremacy* (Boston: Houghton-Mifflin, 1973), p. 40.
3. *United Nations Environment Programme Annual Review* (Nairobi, 1976), p. 10.
4. Ibid.
5. *United Nations Environment Programme Annual Review*, 1978, p. 5.
6. *United Nations Environment Programme Annual Review*, 1976, p. 10.
7. B. H. Svensson and R. Soderlund, eds., *Nitrogen, Phosphorus and Sulphur—Global Cycles* (Stockholm: Swedish Natural Science Research Council, 1976), p. 24.
8. Ibid., p. 42.
9. Ibid., p. 66.
10. United Nations Food and Agricultural Organization, *Monitoring for the Assessment of Selected Critical Environmental Problems Related to Agricultural and Land Use Practices* (Rome: FAO/UNEP, 1976), pp. 24-25.
11. United Nations Food and Agricultural Organization, *Effects of Intensive Fertilizer Use on the Human Environment* (Rome: FAO, 1972), p. 6.
12. Daniel Grosjean, *Nitrogenous Air Pollutants: Chemical and Bio-*

logical Implications (Ann Arbor: Ann Arbor Science Publishers, 1979), p. 340.

13. Great Britain, Department of the Environment, Control Unit on Environmental Pollution, *Chlorofluorocarbons and Their Effect on Stratospheric Ozone* (London: Her Majesty's Stationery Office, 1976), p. 2. For further study on this subject, with particular emphasis on the emissions of nitrogen oxides from inorganic fertilizers, see Machta, *The Ozone Depletion Problem.*

14. *United Nations Environment Programme Annual Review,* 1976, p. 20.

15. United Nations, Conference on Desertification, Nairobi, 1977, *Desertification: Its Causes and Consequences.*

16. For a complete discussion on this subject, see Erik P. Eckholm, *Losing Ground: Environmental Stress and World Food Prospects* (New York: Norton, 1976); Nigel Smith, "Wood: An Ancient Fuel with a New Future," *Worldwatch Paper 42* (Washington, D.C.: Worldwatch Institute, 1981); and Erik P. Eckholm and Lester R. Brown, "Spreading Deserts — The Hand of Man." *Worldwatch Paper 13.*

17. *United Nations Environment Programme Annual Review,* 1981, p. 5.

18. Gene Marine and Judith Van Allen, *Food Pollution: The Violation of Inner Ecology* (New York: Holt, Rinehart, and Winston, 1972), p. 9.

19. See ibid., pp. 38-97 for a fuller discussion of chemical additives in our food.

20. U.S. Department of Agriculture, Soil Conservation Service, *Conquest of the Land through Seven Thousand Years,* Agricultural Bulletin No. 99 (Washington, D.C.: U.S. Government Printing Office, 1953, 1975, and 1978).

21. Ibid.

22. Ibid.

Chapter 2

1. See United Nations World Food Council, *Toward a World without Hunger: Progress and Prospects for Completing the Unfinished Agenda of the World Food Conference* (WFC/1979/3, 23 March 1979).

2. Lynn Adkins, "Enough Food for All?" *Dun's Review* (April 1981), p. 94.

3. Charles P. Lutz, "U.S. Food and World Needs: Four Fallacies," in Lutz, *Farming the Lord's Land* (Minneapolis: Augsburg, 1980), pp. 14-19.

4. "Grain Becomes a Weapon," *Time* (January 21, 1980), p. 23.

5. National Agricultural Lands Study, Interim Report Number 3: *Farm Land and Energy* (Washington, D.C., 1980), p. 14.

6. "Export Crops, Import Trouble," *Los Angeles Times* (September 8, 1981), part II, p. 6.
7. Ibid.
8. See National Agricultural Lands Study, Interim Report Number 5: *America's Agricultural Land Base in 1977*, p. 14. For further discussion on the discrepancies of statistical studies of the nation's cropland, see National Agricultural Lands Study, Interim Report Number 1: *The Program of Study*, pp. 10-12; Interim Report Number 3: *Farm Land and Energy*, pp. 6-7. Interim Report Number 2: *Agricultural Land Data Sheet*, in chart form, is a breakdown by region and states of cropland statistics and definitions of the National Agricultural Lands Study.
9. National Agricultural Lands Study, Interim Report Number 5: *America's Agricultural Land Base in 1977*, p. 6.
10. Ibid., p. 8.
11. Peter J. Ognibene, "Vanishing Farmlands Selling out the Soil," *Saturday Review* (May 1980), p. 29.
12. Roger Blobaum, "The Loss of Agricultural Land," in Richard D. Rodefeld *et al.*, *Change in Rural America* (St. Louis: Mosby, 1978), p. 392.
13. National Agricultural Lands Study, Interim Report Number 5: *America's Agricultural Land Base in 1977*, pp. 8-9.
14. Ibid., p. 14.
15. Ibid.
16. Ibid., p. 15.
17. National Agricultural Lands Study, Interim Report Number 4: *Soil Degradation*, p. 18.
18. Ibid., p. 19.
19. Dr. Hugh Hammond Bennett quoted in ibid., p. 20.
20. David Pimentel *et al.*, "Land Degradation: Effects on Food and Energy Resources," *Science* 194 (October 8, 1976), p. 150.
21. Lester R. Brown, "The Worldwide Loss of Cropland," *Worldwatch Paper 24* (Washington, D.C.: Worldwatch Institute, 1978), p. 24.
22. See Donald Worster, *Dust Bowl: The Southern Plains in the 1930s* (New York: Oxford University Press, 1982).
23. Wes Jackson, *New Roots for Agriculture* (San Francisco: Friends of the Earth, 1980).
24. Bob Bergland, *Face the Nation*, CBS, November 26, 1978.
25. National Agricultural Lands Study, Interim Report Number 4: *Soil Degradation*, p. 20.
26. Ibid.
27. Ibid., p. 28.
28. Ibid., p. 29.
29. Ibid.
30. See R. Neil Sampson, "The Ethical Dimension of Farmland

Protection," in Max Schnept, ed., *Farmland, Food, and the Future* (Ankeny, Iowa: Soil Conservation Society of America, 1980).

31. National Agricultural Lands Study, Interim Report Number 4: *Soil Degradation*, p. 30.
32. "The Losing of America," Advertisement (Emmaus, Pa.: Rodale, 1980).
33. National Agricultural Lands Study, Interim Report Number 4: *Soil Degradation*, p. 36.
34. See San Joaquin Valley Interagency Drainage Program, *Agricultural Drainage and Salt Management in San Joaquin Valley* (Fresno, Calif., 1979), 1.1-1.3.
35. Ibid., 3.6.
36. Ibid.
37. Schwarz, Joel, "Farming's Salty Solution," *American Way* (March 1980), p. 89.
38. National Agricultural Lands Study, Interim Report Number 4: *Soil Degradation*, p. 37.
39. Ibid., p. 38. See also United States, Council on Environmental Quality, *Environmental Quality—1979* (Washington, D.C.: U.S. Government Printing Office, 1980).
40. W. B. Voorhees, "Soil Tilth Deterioration under Row Cropping in the Northern Corn Belt," *Journal of Soil and Water Conservation* (July-August 1979): 184.
41. Ibid., p. 186.
42. Ibid.
43. Ognibene, p. 29.
44. Adkins, p. 99.
45. National Agricultural Lands Study, Interim Report Number 3: *Farm Land and Energy*, p. 11.
46. Ibid.
47. Ibid., p. 12.
48. Ibid., p. 21.
49. Ibid.
50. Ibid., p. 22.
51. Ibid.
52. Ibid., p. 23.
53. Ibid., p. 28.
54. Jackson, p. 31.
55. Ibid.
56. Norman Myers, *The Sinking Ark: A New Look at the Problem of Disappearing Species* (New York: Pergamon Press, 1979).
57. Ibid., p. ix.
58. Wilson Clark, "U.S. Agriculture Is Growing Trouble as Well as Crops," *Smithsonian* (January 1975): 64.
59. Ibid.

Chapter 3

1. National Agricultural Lands Study, Interim Report Number 4: *Soil Degradation*, p. 39.
2. Ibid.
3. National Research Council, Committee on Agricultural Production Efficiency, *Agricultural Production Efficiency* (Washington, D.C.: National Academy of Science, 1975), p. 101.
4. Ibid.
5. See Arthur A. Millecan, *A Survey and Assessment of Air Pollution Damage to California Vegetation 1970 through 1974* (Sacramento: State of California Department of Food and Agriculture, 1976).
6. National Agricultural Lands Study, Interim Report Number 4: *Soil Degradation*, p. 40.
7. Ibid.
8. Jackson, p. 29.
9. United States Congress, Senate, *The Development and Allocation of Scarce World Resources*, 94th Cong., 1st sess., 94-95, pp. 196-197.
10. National Agricultural Lands Study, Interim Report Number 4: *Soil Degradation*, p. 34.
11. "The Browning of America," *Newsweek* (February 23, 1981), p. 26.
12. Ibid., p. 27.
13. National Agricultural Lands Study, Interim Report Number 4: *Soil Degradation*, p. 34.
14. John Fischer, *From the High Plains* (New York: Harper & Row, 1978).
15. Ibid., pp. 171-173.
16. Ibid., p. 179.
17. National Agricultural Lands Study, Interim Report Number 4: *Soil Degradation*, p. 34.
18. "The Browning of America," p. 37.
19. Toole, K. Ross, *The Rape of the Great Plains* (Boston: Little, Brown, 1976), pp. 18-20.
20. Jackson, p. 31.
21. For a full discussion, see Harold W. Bernard Jr., *The Greenhouse Effect* (Cambridge, Mass.: Ballinger, 1980); George M. Woodwell *et al.*, "The Carbon Dioxide Question," *Scientific American* (January 1978), pp. 34-43.
22. Bernard, *The Greenhouse Effect*.
23. Ibid., p. 1.
24. See Woodwell, pp. 34-43.
25. Bernard, p. 7.
26. Ibid., p. 13.
27. *Los Angeles Times*, April 23, 1983, Part I, p. 14.
28. Woodwell, p. 34.

29. John Gribbin, "When the Climate Becomes Too Hot to Handle,"
    Guardian (London) (February 26, 1971), p. 13.
30. Ibid.
31. Ibid.
32. Bernard, p. 18.
33. Stephen H. Schneider, "On the Carbon Dioxide-Climate Confu-
    sion," *Journal of the Atmospheric Science* 32 (1975): 2060,
    quoted in Bernard, *The Greenhouse Effect,* p. 20.
34. Ibid.

Chapter 4

1. Denis Hayes, *Rays of Hope: The Transition to a Post-Petroleum
    World* (New York: W. W. Norton, 1977), p. 97.
 2. "Grain Becomes a Weapon," p. 14.
 3. David and Marcia Pimentel, *Food, Energy and Society,* (New
    York: John Wiley & Sons, 1979), p. 137; and Hayes, *Rays of
    Hope,* p. 92.
 4. Pimentel, *Food, Energy and Society,* p. 137.
 5. Jackson, p. 25.
 6. Ibid.
 7. Pimentel, *Food, Energy and Society,* p. 8.
 8. Ibid., p. 16.
 9. Ibid., p. 7.
10. Ibid., pp. 8, 137.
11. Ibid., pp. 120-121.
12. Hayes, p. 31.
13. Ibid., p. 91.
14. Ibid., p. 93.
15. Blobaum, "The Loss of Agricultural Land," in Rodefeld, p. 396.
16. Pimentel, *Food, Energy and Society,* p. 27.
17. Hayes, p. 103.
18. Jackson, p. 12.
19. Pimentel, *Food, Energy and Society,* p. 143.
20. For a thorough analysis of fossil-fuel energy resource esti-
    mates and time projections, see Lester R. Brown, "Population
    Policies for a New Economic Era," *Worldwatch Paper 53*
    (Washington, D.C.: Worldwatch Institute, 1983).
21. See Lutz, *Farming the Lord's Land.* For a most authoritative
    and exhaustively researched study on U.S. rural communities,
    the family farm, and agribusiness, see Ingolf Vogeler, *The Myth
    of the Family Farm: Agribusiness Dominance of U.S. Agricul-
    ture* (Boulder, Colo.: Westview Press, 1981).
22. Robert Riedel and Jon Wefald, "Strengthening Rural Communi-
    ties," in Lutz, *Farming the Lord's Land,* p. 107.
23. See "Grain Becomes a Weapon," p. 14. "Farms grew larger and

the number of people on them dwindled . . . to less than 5% of today's population (1981) as compared with 23% in 1940."
24. Riedel and Wefald, p. 109.
25. Ibid.
26. Ibid., p. 110.
27. For a provocative discussion about this matter, see Dieter T. Hessel, ed., *The Agricultural Mission of Churches and Land-Grant Universities* (Ames: Iowa State University Press, 1979).
28. W. C. Lowdermilk, *Conquest of the Land through Seven Thousand Years.*
29. For substantial studies on these issues, see Michael Perelman, *Farming for Profit in a Hungry World: Capital and the Crisis in Agriculture* (Montclair: Allanheld, 1978); John A. Young and Jan M. Newton, *Capitalism and Human Obsolescence: Corporate Control Versus Individual Survival in Rural America* (Montclair: Allanheld, 1980); Wendell Berry, *The Unsettling of America: Culture & Agriculture* (San Francisco: Sierra Club Books, 1977); and Frances Moore Lappé and Joseph Collins, *Food First: Beyond the Myth of Scarcity* (New York: Ballantine, 1979).
30. Riedel and Wefald, p. 110.
31. Jerry Moles, "Structure and Meaning in American Agriculture," paper.
32. Young, *Capitalism and Human Obsolescence*, p. 134, quoting from the San Francisco *Sunday Examiner and Chronicle*, March 20, 1977.
33. *Capitalism and Human Obsolescence*, p. 157.
34. Paul Johnson, "Family Farming: Does It Serve the Common Good?" in Lutz, *Farming the Lord's Land*, p. 48.
35. Tom Dybdahl, "America the Bountiful" (Emmaus, Pa.: Rodale Press, 1981), paper.
36. Jackson, p. 1.
37. Don F. Hadwiger, *The Politics of Agricultural Research* (Lincoln: University of Nebraska Press, 1982).

Chapter 5

1. Donald Imsland, *Celebrate the Earth* (Minneapolis: Augsburg, 1971), p. 61. See also David Tobin Asselin, "The Notion of Dominion in Genesis 1–3," *Biblical Quarterly* 16 (July 1954): 293; Richard Cartwright Austin, "Toward Environmental Theology," *Drew Gateway* (Winter 1977), p. 7; Nahum M. Sarna, *Understanding Genesis* (New York: McGraw-Hill, 1966), p. 15; and Gerhard von Rad, *Genesis: A Commentary* (Philadelphia: Westminster Press, 1973), p. 59.
2. John D. Davies, *Beginning Now: A Christian Exploration of the*

First Three Chapters of Genesis (Philadelphia: Fortress Press, 1971), p. 102.

3. Bruce D. Naidoff, "A Man to Work the Soil: A New Interpretation of Genesis 2–3," *Journal for the Study of the Old Testament* (January 1978), p. 4.

4. Dietrich Bonhoeffer, *Creation and Temptation* (London: SCM Press, 1966), p. 38.

5. H. Paul Santmire, *Brother Earth: Nature, God, and Ecology in Time of Crisis* (New York: Thomas Nelson, 1970), pp. 84-85.

6. B. W. Anderson, "Human Dominion over Nature," in *Biblical Studies in Contemporary Thought*, ed. by Miriam Ward (Somerville: Greeno, Hadden, 1975), p. 45.

7. Richard A. Baer Jr., "Land Misuse: A Theological Concern," *Christian Century* (October 12, 1977), p. 1240.

8. B. W. Anderson, "Creation," in *The Interpreter's Dictionary of the Bible*, vol. 1 (Nashville: Abingdon, 1962), p. 728.

9. Imsland, p. 43.

10. Steck, Odil Hannes, *World and Environment* (Nashville: Abingdon, 1980), pp. 75-77.

11. Plastaras, James, *Creation and Covenant* (Encino, Calif., Glencoe, 1968).

12. Steck, p. 71.

13. Ibid., p. 86.

14. Ibid., p. 103.

15. Anderson, "Creation," p. 729.

16. Anderson, "Human Dominion over Nature," p. 61.

17. H. Schwarz, "Humanity as God's Image in Evolutionary Perspective," *Theologische Zeitschrift* 34:334-344.

18. Imsland, *Celebrate the Earth*, p. 61. See also Asselin, "The Notion of Dominion in Genesis 1–3," p. 298; Austin, "Toward Environmental Theology," p. 7; Sarna, *Understanding Genesis*, p. 15; and Von Rad, *Genesis*, p. 59.

19. Asselin, p. 293.

20. Austin, p. 7.

21. Steck, p. 112.

22. Ibid., p. 259.

23. Ibid., p. 229.

24. Ibid., p. 264.

25. Ibid., pp. 296-298.

26. Ibid.

Chapter 6

1. Richard Merrill, ed., *Radical Agriculture* (New York: Harper & Row, 1976), p. 284.

2. The concept of "justice, participation, and sustainability" is the climax of more than 40 years of ecumenical effort to articulate the meaning of the responsible global society. These norma-

tive guidelines were the focus of the World Council of Churches conference on "Faith, Science and the Future," held at the Massachusetts Institute of Technology, Cambridge, July 12-24, 1979.
3. William T. Blackstone, "The Search for an Environmental Ethic," in *Matters of Life and Death,* ed. by Tom Regan (Philadelphia: Temple University Press, 1980), p. 327.
4. See E. F. Schumacher, *Small Is Beautiful* (New York: Harper & Row, 1975) for the development of the problem theme that natural resources in the industrialized world are considered as income resources.
5. Albert Schweitzer, *Reverence for Life* (New York: Holt, Rinehart, and Winston, 1965), p. 33.
York: Holt, Rinehart, and Winston, 1965), p. 33.
6. *Faith and Science in an Unjust World* (Geneva: World Council of Churches, 1980), vol. 1, p. 225.
7. Mische, Gerald and Patricia, *Toward a Human World Order: Beyond the National Security Straitjacket* (New York: Paulist Press, 1977), p. 169.
8. *Faith and Science in an Unjust World,* Vol. 1, p. 27.
9. See Mische, *Toward a Human World Order.*
10. W. H. Murdy, "Anthropocentrism: A Modern Version," *Science* (March 28, 1975), p. 1169.
11. See Herman E. Daly, "The Ecological and Moral Necessity for Limiting Economic Growth," in *Faith and Science in an Unjust World,* vol. 1, pp. 212-220.
12. Ebeling, p. 393.
13. René Dubos, *The Wooing of Earth* (New York: Scribner, 1981), p. 175.
14. Ibid., p. 244.
15. Ibid.
16. Ibid., p. 161.
17. Ibid., p. 108.
18. Ibid., p. 152.
19. *Faith and Science in an Unjust World,* vol. 2, p. 70.
20. Richard Cartwright Austin, "Three Axioms for Land Use," *Christian Century* (October 12, 1977), p. 915.

Chapter 7

1. J. Sholto Douglas and Robert A. de J. Hart, *Forest Farming: Towards a Solution to Problems of World Hunger and Conservation,* rev. ed., (London: Watkins, 1980), p. ix.
2. Ibid., p. 9.
3. Richard St. Barbe Baker, "The Skin of the Earth," *Warm Wind* (Spring 1980), p. 16.
4. Ibid., p. 17.

5. Joseph Russell Smith, *Tree Crops: A Permanent Agriculture* (New York: Harcourt, Brace, 1929).
6. For the story of the evolution of the concept of tree farming, see Douglas, *Forest Farming*, p. 1.
7. Ibid., p. 19.
8. Ibid., p. 45.
9. Ibid., p. 46.
10. Ibid.
11. Ibid., p. 23.
12. Ibid., p. 86.
13. Ibid., p. 159.
14. Jackson, p. 5.
15. Ibid., pp. 137-154.
16. Ibid., p. 132.
17. David Hopcraft, "Productivity Comparison between Thompson's Gazelle and Cattle, and Their Relation to the Eco-system in Kenya," Ph.D. dissertation, Cornell University, 1975, p. 1.
18. Ibid., p. 179.
19. Ibid.
20. Ibid.

Chapter 8

1. Erik P. Eckholm, *Down to Earth* (New York: W. W. Norton & Co., 1982), p. 209.
2. Dennis Gabor and Umberto Colombo, *Beyond the Age of Waste: A Report to the Club of Rome* (New York: Pergamon Press, 1981), p. 157.
3. S. H. Wittwer, "The Next Generation of Agricultural Research," *Science* 199 (January 27, 1978): 375.
4. Ibid.
5. Gabor, p. 199.
6. Gary A. Strobel, "A New Grants Program in Agriculture," *Science* 199 (March 3, 1978): 935.
7. Bede N. Okigbo, "Plant Technology in Today's World and Problems of Continued Widespread Adaption in Less Developed Countries," in *Proceedings, the World Food Conference of 1976* (Ames: Iowa State University Press, 1977), p. 464.
8. Ibid.
9. R. Neil Sampson, *Farmland or Wasteland* (Emmaus, Pa.: Rodale Press, 1981), pp. 334-336.
10. National Agricultural Lands Study, *The Protection of Farmland: A Reference Guidebook for State and Local Governments* (Washington, D.C., 1982).
11. Ibid., p. 16.
12. Ann L. Strong, *Land Banking: European Reality, American Prospect* (Baltimore: Johns Hopkins University Press, 1979).

13. National Agricultural Lands Study, *The Protection of Farmland: A Reference Guidebook for State and Local Governments,* pp. 281-282.

Chapter 9

1. Walter Brueggemann, *In Man We Trust* (Atlanta: John Knox Press, 1972).
2. Ibid., p. 113.

Bibliography

Adkins, Lynn. "Enough Food for All?" *Dun's Review,* April 1981, pp. 94-102.

Anderson, B. W. "Creation." In *The Interpreter's Dictionary of the Bible,* edited by George A. Buttrick. Nashville: Abingdon, 1962.

Anderson, B. W. "Human Dominion over Nature." In *Biblical Studies in Contemporary Thought,* edited by Miriam Ward. Somerville: Greeno Hadden, 1975.

Asselin, David Tobin. "The Notion of Dominion in Genesis 1-3." *Biblical Quarterly* 16 (July 1954): 277-294.

Austin, Richard Cartwright. "Three Axioms for Land Use." *Christian Century,* 12 October 1977.

Austin, Richard Cartwright. "Toward Environmental Theology." *Drew Gateway* 48 (Winter 1977): 1-14.

Baer, Richard A. Jr. "Land Misuse: A Theological Concern." *Christian Century,* 12 October 1977.

Baker, Richard St. Barbe. "The Skin of the Earth." *Warm Wind,* Spring 1980.

Bernard, Harold W. Jr., *The Greenhouse Effect.* New York: Harper & Row, 1981.

Berry, Wendell. *The Unsettling of America: Culture and Agriculture.* San Francisco: Sierra Club, 1977.

Blackstone, William T. "The Search for an Environmental Ethic." In *Matters of Life and Death,* edited by Tom Regan. New York: Random, 1980.

Bonhoeffer, Dietrich. *Creation and Temptation.* London: SCM, 1966.

Brown, Lester R. "Population Policies for a New Economic Era."

Worldwatch Paper 53. Washington, D.C.: Worldwatch Institute, 1983.

Brown, Lester R. "The Worldwide Loss of Cropland." *Worldwatch Paper 24.* Washington, D.C.: Worldwatch Institute, 1978.

"The Browning of America." *Newsweek,* 23 February 1981.

Brueggemann, Walter. *In Man We Trust: The Neglected Side of Biblical Faith.* Atlanta: John Knox Press, 1972.

Bryson, Reid A. and Murray, Thomas J. *Climates of Hunger: Mankind and the World's Changing Weather.* Madison: University of Wisconsin Press, 1977.

CBS. "Face the Nation," 26 November 1978. Interview with Bob Bergland.

Clark, Wilson. "U.S. Agriculture Is Growing Trouble as Well as Crops." *Smithsonian* 5 (January 1975): 59-64.

Davies, John D. *Beginning Now: A Christian Exploration of the First Three Chapters of Genesis.* Philadelphia: Fortress, 1971. Out of print.

Douglas, J. Sholto and Hart, Robert A. de J. *Forest Farming: Towards a Solution to Problems of World Hunger and Conservation.* Rev. ed. London: Watkins, 1980.

Dubos, René. *The Wooing of Earth.* New York: Scribner, 1981.

Dybdahl, Tom. "America the Bountiful." A research paper for the Cornucopia Project. Emmaus, Pa.: Rodale, 1981.

Ebeling, Walter. *The Fruited Plain: The Story of American Agriculture.* Berkeley: Univ. of Calif., 1980.

Eckholm, Erik. *Down to Earth: Environment and Human Needs.* New York: Norton, 1982.

Eckholm, Erik P. *Losing Ground: Environmental Stress and World Food Prospects.* New York: Pergamon, 1978.

Eckholm, Erik and Brown, Lester R. "Spreading Deserts — The Hand of Man." *Worldwatch Paper 13.* Washington, D.C.: Worldwatch Institute, 1977.

"Export Crops, Import Trouble." *Los Angeles Times,* 8 September 1981, part II, p. 6.

Faith and Science in an Unjust World. Report of the World Council of Churches Conference on Faith, Science and the Future, Massachusetts Institute of Technology, 12-24 July 1979. Vol. 1: Plenary Presentations, edited by Roger L. Shinn. Vol. 2: Reports and Recommendations, edited by Paul Abrecht. Geneva: World Council of Churches, 1980.

Fischer, John. *From the High Plains.* New York: Harper & Row, 1978.

Gabor, Dennis and Colombo, Umberto. *Beyond the Age of Waste: A Report to the Club of Rome.* New York: Pergamon, 1981.

"Grain Becomes a Weapon." *Time,* 21 January 1980.

Great Britain. Department of the Environment. Control Unit on Environmental Pollution. *Chlorofluorocarbons and Their Effect on Stratospheric Ozone.* Pollution Paper Number 5. London: Her Majesty's Stationery Office, 1976.

Gribbin, John. "When the Climate Becomes Too Hot to Handle." *Guardian* (London), 26 February 1981.

Grosjean, Daniel, ed. *Nitrogenous Air Pollutants: Chemical and Biological Implications.* Ann Arbor: Ann Arbor Science Publishers, 1979.

Hadwiger, Don F. *The Politics of Agricultural Research.* Lincoln: University of Nebraska Press, 1982.

Hayes, Denis. *Rays of Hope: The Transition to a Post-Petroleum World.* A Worldwatch Institute Book. New York: Norton, 1977.

Hessel, Dieter T., ed. *The Agricultural Mission of Churches and Land-Grant Universities: A Report of an Informal Consultation.* Ames: Iowa State Univ., 1979.

Hopcraft, David. "Productivity Comparison between Thompson's Gazelle and Cattle, and Their Relation to the Eco-System in Kenya." Ph.D. dissertation, Cornell University, 1975.

Imsland, Donald. *Celebrate the Earth.* Minneapolis: Augsburg, 1971. Out of print.

Jackson, Wes. *New Roots for Agriculture.* Andover, Mass.: Brick, 1980.

Lappé, Frances Moore and Collins, Joseph. *Food First: Beyond the Myth of Scarcity.* New York: Ballantine, 1979.

Los Angeles Times, 23 April 1983, part I, p. 14.

Livingston, John A. *One Cosmic Instant: Man's Fleeting Supremacy.* Boston: Houghton-Mufflin. Out of print.

"The Losing of America." Advertisement. Emmaus, Pa.: Rodale, 1980.

Lutz, Charles P., ed. *Farming the Lord's Land: Christian Perspectives on American Agriculture.* Minneapolis: Augsburg, 1980.

Marine, Gene and Van Allen, Judith. *Food Pollution: The Violation of Inner Ecology.* New York: Holt, Rinehart & Winston, 1972. Out of print.

Merrill, Richard, ed. *Radical Agriculture.* New York: New York University, 1976.

Millecan, Arthur A. *A Survey and Assessment of Air Pollution*

Damage to California Vegetation 1970 through 1974. Sacramento: State of California Department of Food and Agriculture, 1976.

Mische, Gerald and Patricia. *Toward a Human World Order: Beyond the National Security Straitjacket.* New York: Paulist, 1977.

Moles, Jerry. "Structure and Meaning in American Agriculture." Paper prepared for Symposium on Farm Structure and Rural Policy, Iowa State University, Ames, Iowa, 20-22 October 1980.

Murdy, W. H. "Anthropocentrism: A Modern Version." *Science* 187 (March 28, 1975) : 1168-1172.

Myers, Norman. *The Sinking Ark: A New Look at the Problem of Disappearing Species.* New York: Pergamon, 1979.

Naidoff, Bruce D. "A Man to Work the Soil: A New Interpretation of Genesis 2-3." *Journal for the Study of the Old Testament,* Issue 5 (January 1978) : 2-14.

National Agricultural Lands Study. Interim Report No. 1: *The Program of Study.* Interim Report No. 2: *Agricultural Land Data Sheet.* Interim Report No. 3: *Farm Land and Energy: Conflicts in the Making,* by W. Wendell Fletcher. Interim Report No. 4: *Soil Degradation: Effects on Agricultural Productivity,* prepared by the National Association of Conservation Districts. Interim Report No. 5: *America's Agricultural Land Base in 1977.* Washington, D.C.: National Agricultural Lands Study, 1980.

National Agricultural Lands Study. *The Protection of Farmland: A Reference Guidebook for State and Local Governments.* Washington, D.C.: National Agricultural Lands Study, 1982.

National Research Council. Committee on Agricultural Production Efficiency. *Agricultural Production Efficiency.* Washington, D.C.: National Academy of Science, 1975.

Ognibene, Peter J. "Vanishing Farmlands Selling out the Soil." *Saturday Review,* May 1980.

Okigbo, Bede N. "Plant Technology in Today's World and Problems of Continued Widespread Adaption in Less Developed Countries." In *Proceedings, the World Food Conference of 1976.* Ames: Iowa State University, 1977.

Perelman, Michael. *Farming for Profit in a Hungry World: Capital and the Crisis in Agriculture.* LandMark Studies. Montclair: Allanheld, 1978.

Pimentel, David and Marcia. *Food, Energy and Society.* Resource and Environmental Science Series. New York: Halsted, 1979.

Pimentel, David et al. "Land Degradation: Effects on Food and Energy Resources." *Science* 194 (October 8, 1976): 149-155.

Plastaras, James. *Creation and Covenant.* Encino, Calif.: Glencoe, 1968.

Rodefeld, Richard D. *et al*, eds. *Change in Rural America: Causes, Consequences, and Alternatives.* St. Louis: Mosby, 1978.

Sampson, R. Neil. "The Ethical Dimension of Farmland Protection." In *Farmland, Food, and the Future.* Edited by Max Schnept. Ankeny, Iowa: Soil Conservation Society of America, 1980.

Sampson, R. Neil. *Farmland or Wasteland: A Time to Choose.* Emmaus, Pa.: Rodale, 1981.

San Joaquin Valley Interagency Drainage Program. *Agricultural Drainage and Salt Management in San Joaquin Valley.* Final Report, including Recommended Plan and First-Stage Environmental Impact Report. 2 vols. Sponsored by United States Department of the Interior, Bureau of Reclamation; California Department of Water Resources; California State Water Resources Control Board. Fresno, Calif.: San Joaquin Valley Interagency Drainage Program, 1979.

Santmire, H. Paul. *Brother Earth: Nature, God and Ecology in Time of Crisis.* New York: Thomas Nelson, 1970. Out of print.

Sarna, Nahum M. *Understanding Genesis: The Heritage of Biblical Israel.* New York: Shocken, 1970.

Schneider, Stephen H., with Lynne E. Mesirow. *The Genesis Strategy: Climate and Global Survival.* New York: Plenum, 1976.

Schumacher, E. F. *Good Work.* New York: Harper & Row, 1980.

Schumacher, E. F. *Small Is Beautiful: Economics As If People Mattered.* New York: Harper & Row, 1975.

Schwarz, H. "Humanity as God's Image in Evolutionary Perspective." *Theologische Zeitschrift* 34 (November/December 1978): 334-344.

Schwarz, Joel. "Farming's Salty Solution." *American Way,* March 1980.

Schweitzer, Albert. *Reverence for Life.* New York: Pilgrim, 1969.

Smith, Joseph Russell. *Tree Crops: A Permanent Agriculture.* New York: Harcourt, Brace, 1929. Out of print.

Smith, Nigel. "Wood: An Ancient Fuel with a New Future." *Worldwatch 42.* Washington, D.C.: Worldwatch Institute, 1981.

Steck, Odil Hannes. *World and Environment.* Biblical Encounters Series. Margaret Kohl, trans. Nashville: Abingdon, 1980.

Strobel, Gary A. "A New Grants Program in Agriculture." *Science* 199 (March 3, 1978): 935.

Strong, Ann L. *Land Banking: European Reality, American Prospect.* Baltimore: Johns Hopkins University, 1979.

Svensson, B. H. and Soderlund, R., eds. *Nitrogen, Phosphorus and Sulphur—Global Cycles.* Report from a project on biogeochemical cycles initiated by the Scientific Committee on Problems of the

Environment (SCOPE) of ICSU, arranged by the Swedish SCOPE Committee of the Royal Swedish Academy of Sciences. Stockholm: Swedish Natural Science Research Council, 1976.

Toole, K. Ross. *The Rape of the Great Plains: Northwest America, Cattle and Coal.* Boston: Little, Brown, 1976.

United Nations. Conference on Desertification, Nairobi, 1977. *Desertification: Its Causes and Consequences.* Compiled and edited by the Secretariat of the United Nations Conference on Desertification, Nairobi, Kenya, 29 August–9 September 1977. New York: Pergamon, 1977.

United Nations Food and Agricultural Organization. *Effects of Intensive Fertilizer Use on the Human Environment.* Rome: Unipub, 1972.

United Nations Food and Agricultural Organization. *Monitoring for the Assessment of Selected Critical Environmental Problems Related to Agricultural and Land Use Practices.* Rome: FAO/UNEP Government Expert Group on Environmental Monitoring of Soil and Vegetative Cover, 1976.

United Nations World Food Council. *Toward a World without Hunger: Progress and Prospects for Completing the Unfinished Agenda of the World Food Conference.* Report by the Executive Director on the 5th Ministerial Session. WFC/1979/3, 23 March 1979.

United Nations Environment Programme Annual Review. Nairobi: United Nations Environment Programme, 1976.

U.S. Congress. Senate. *The Development and Allocation of Scarce World Resources.* 94th Cong., 1st sess., 94-95.

U.S. Council on Environmental Quality. *Environmental Quality— 1979.* The Tenth Report of the Council on Environmental Quality. Washington, D.C.: U.S. Government Printing Office, 1980.

U.S. Department of Agriculture. Soil Conservation Service. *Conquest of the Land through Seven Thousand Years.* Agricultural Information Bulletin No. 99. Washington, D.C.: U.S. Government Printing Office, 1953, 1975, and 1978.

Vogeler, Ingolf. *The Myth of the Family Farm: Agribusiness Dominance of U.S. Agriculture.* Boulder, Colo.: Westview, 1981.

Von Rad, Gerhard. *Genesis: A Commentary.* Philadelphia: Westminster, 1973.

Voorhees, W. B. "Soil Tilth Deterioration under Row Cropping in the Northern Corn Belt: Influence of Tillage and Wheel Traffic." *Journal of Soil and Water Conservation* (July-August 1979): 184-186.

Westermann, Claus. *Genesis 1-11: A Commentary*. Minneapolis: Augsburg, 1984.

Wittwer, S. H. "The Next Generation of Agricultural Research." *Science* 199 (January 27, 1978) : 375.

Woodwell, George M. "The Carbon Dioxide Question." *Scientific American* 238 (January 1978) : 34-43.

Worster, Donald. *Dust Bowl: The Southern Plains in the 1930s*. New York: Oxford, 1982.

Young, John A. and Newton, Jan M. *Capitalism and Human Obsolescence: Corporate Control Versus Individual Survival in Rural America*. Montclair: Allanheld, 1980.